# THE WAY
# of
# FUZZY FAITH

### Michael Quillin

1

## DEDICATION

To all of the students who taught me.

And to Lil, whose faith in me and this
project was never fuzzy.

# ACKNOWLEDGMENTS

To all those who encouraged me in this project, especially my first enthusiastic readers: Larry Siewert, Pat Fennessy, Jack Quillin, Maureen Monk and Lee Lechtenberg. They were generous enough to put aside their critical views and give me the confidence to go forward.

To Kathy Cushman, for her careful proof-reading and prescient insights.

And to Andy Bartlett, who allayed my fears of self-publishing and convinced me I could actually get this into book form.

To Lil Zadra, for the cover photograph.

All Bible quotes are from the New American Bible translation.

# CONTENTS

MICHAEL QUILLIN

# 1 METHOD

When I was a kid I assumed that all adults told the truth. If I asked a question, I figured that whatever adult was answering it was telling the truth. If I asked a question about faith, it was automatic that the nun or priest or parent or grown-up would tell me the truth. In those days faith questions were different than they are now. I remember a nun being confronted with the theological poser of whether you broke your Communion fast if you ate a fingernail accidentally. (Two years running, I swear, someone had that question, probably the same kid who had an issue with nail chewing, and when the answer was different each year, I knew something was up.)

As I got older I realized that all adults didn't answer those faith questions honestly. Oh, it's not that they were dishonest adults answering the questions, it's just that they didn't understand the question properly. They didn't answer what they really believed, they answered what they wanted to believe. Yes, it was wrong to miss Mass on Sunday, to swear, to tell a falsehood. Did they believe that? Well, yes, they wanted to believe that, and did they believe that in all situations? No, not always, there were extenuating circumstances. So, is it wrong? Well, yes, but . . .

I have tried in this book to answer all questions according to what I do believe in my daily life, and not what I feel I should say on any given topic. I have tried to avoid the situation where I am compelled to say something so that I don't give a bad example or cause someone else not to believe. My thoughts on these topics are what I have come to know and understand over a lifetime of trying to live my faith honestly, whether those conclusions end up being orthodox or heretical.

Do you believe or not? The question of faith is often characterized in just such a fashion, and there is a lot to justify that approach. I love it! It's so dramatic. Belief or unbelief. Are you with me or not? The sheep and the goats. CHOOSE! It is the existential decision of your life!

But it just doesn't seem to square with my lived experience. Sometimes I do things that seem very Christian and other times . . . Well, other times, it just seems like I forget that Jesus is in the equation. I commit myself to prayer, and don't have a moment where I say, No, I won't pray! I just have moments strung together into days where I forget to pray or forget that I made the decision to pray.

So, yes, you can frame the question of faith into a strict all or nothing decision to believe or not to believe. After all, Jesus seems to have put it just so starkly when he told his followers that those who were not for him were against him. Although in another account, it's those who aren't against him who are for him, a big difference in my book, something I will visit again later.

But a lot of the time, it doesn't feel like such a dramatic split captures the scene correctly. I don't know if people really believe or reject completely, they seem more to muddle along a chain of positions believing at times and skeptical at others.

I find in my life not a lot of either/or junctures where a leap of faith is required. Much more it is a matter of snail crawls with percentages of faith and unfaith, like the man in the gospel who says, "I believe, help my unbelief."

Fuzzy logic in computer searches has been a huge bonus for those searching for something but aren't quite certain what it is or how it's called. Fuzzy faith, I think, works the same way: it's for people who are searching for something, but they don't quite know what it is. In fact, they may not even be conscious of being on a search for it or missing it, but they are.

If we start with this concept, then, we get at the heart of what I see today. It is becoming less and less a matter of whether you are Catholic or Protestant or Jewish, but rather how much you have seen and accepted and how much just doesn't seem to make any sense to you.

This book is dedicated to those of fuzzy faith, who might have believed once, but don't anymore, might have been raised in a tradition but see little to keep you attached to those ways now. In the famous Parable of the Sower, Jesus talks about the different fates of the seed being sown. One of the results is seed on rocky ground. It does grow, but not for very long. I can't think of any other parable where Jesus spends as much time explaining as he does this one. The seed on rocky ground just doesn't have the depth to grow very much and soon dies. A lot of us are like that seed, I think. We have at times in our lives been animated by Jesus and his message, but then we go on and forget about that message, and soon it is as if we had never heard the message.

A word about method: It would seem that a work of this type would require some scholarship and research in order to present the best insights and approach to this very important subject. I have been the willing or unwilling subject of many erudite talks over the course of my life and I have come to this conclusion. For the sake of this book, what is important is what I remember, what has stayed with me over the years. It is of course impressive to look up a ton of references to back up what I say and to impress you with my scholarship, but that's not really indicative of my lived experience of faith and so not consistent with the aim of this book.

So, as a result, I have hit upon another approach: No research. I intend to do no extra searching through all my years of notes or through the many dusty tomes I have faithfully and fruitlessly carried with me over the years.

There are many reasons for this approach.

First, I'm lazy. I have an aversion to looking through anthologies and indexes hunting down a reference. Once I have read a book I have no ambition to return to it (The Great Gatsby being the exception). All of those highlighters I went through to color those purple passages have gone dry for no good reason. I never went back and reread the notes. Even now, when I have entered the digital age and highlight passages on my Kindle I find that I never go back and reread them.

I also have an aversion to the pose which pretends that all of this stuff resides clearly in my memory. I recall the old New Yorker cartoon of the writer who starts, "As Aristotle said . . ." And then gets up (this is in pre-Internet days) and goes to a shelf of books behind him and comes back writing, "Or was it Homer?" Things flit in and out of my head like spooks in a mansion and to present any more sane picture would be a travesty. I remember various chestnuts of scholarship like "If a tree falls in the forest and no one is there, does it make a sound?" But I don't usually recall the esoteric explanation that followed, so that the end result of someone's long, arduous climb for knowledge ends up being little more than a parlor trick ice-breaker. The results are even more shameful when they incorporate smatterings of other languages. "Ad astra per aspera" etc. In the interest of some basic intellectual honesty I have foresworn the showy bits of learned lore pumped up through romps amid the poppies of Wikipedia. What you get is the same unadorned knowledge you would get from bumping into me at a party.

But the main reason for this approach is more fundamental: If I don't remember it, it didn't really stick with me. No sense going back and finding a lot of esoteric quotes to make me sound learned or to legitimize my views. If I can't recall it on my own, it never really became part of my daily, living world view. I have over the years sat through many brilliant lectures studded with insightful comments and ground-breaking ideas, but a week after the lecture I remained as clueless as before. I have been explained the nature of evil and suffering so that it was clear that suffering could exist alongside a good God, but in a month or two I forgot the exact wording and the clever reasoning and I was back where I was before. Befuddled. I could recommend a few tomes for you; I may even have some sitting at home in my library resting, like Gatsby's library books, uncut and unread.

So my approach is to stick mainly to things that have penetrated the thick hide of my ignorance and nestled in my daily trove of knowledge. These are the things which for better or worse I live by. Obviously, if you desire deeper cogent formulations of the nature of reality you wouldn't be poking around on the lower shelves of literature for a book like this in the first place.

In terms of the organization of this book, it's sort of like Mark Twain's approach to theme: Anyone attempting to find one will be shot. Aside from the first and last chapters, there isn't any compelling reason to read one chapter ahead of another simply because it appears first in the book. The chapters are independent and can be sampled in any order you prefer, depending on your mood or interest at the moment.

So, with that, we begin.

# 2 FUZZY FAITH

In the pursuit of knowledge and other less praiseworthy endeavors on the Internet, the concept of fuzzy logic has revolutionized the way we think. When I first heard the name, I thought it was a joke, an apt description of the way most of us think. There's a brilliant section in Don DeLillo's <u>White Noise</u>, where the family is sitting around having a discussion. It's a far-ranging affair touching on many concepts, but getting none of them exactly right. Everything is close, but not quite right, leading to mass confusion and bewilderment. That was my thought about the idea of fuzzy logic.

And that's not far wrong. Much of the time we hold notions that are partially true and kind of wrong. That's why fuzzy logic is so useful. If we want to know about cyborgs, but can't quite come up with the correct spelling, fuzzy logic helps us out. It knows that many people spell the word with an s or an I and gives us alternatives. It sees the correct in the midst of the errors.

I think that we could use some fuzzy thinking in the area of faith. Almost every discussion of faith I have ever gotten into boils down to a basic either-or dilemma. One side is right or the other. There is no attempt to find what is right in the spelling of cyborg and work from there, but an immediate focus on the offending "si" in it. There is no going forward from that focus. There is no helpful "Did you mean . . ." To help us move forward from one inchoate thought to something more formed and complete. You start with the notion that there might be something beyond this life. Or you start with the idea that there must be some meaning to what we are doing here, some purpose to our existence, and that leads to deeper insight.

Fuzzy faith starts with an incomplete concept. We know it's incomplete, that it needs to be filled in, but the little we know shapes our search, heads us in the proper direction. It's not a claim to having total understanding or a patent on the truth, but that we have some embryonic knowledge that will guide us on our quest. In this sense we are not right or wrong, but on the journey to find the truth. Fuzzy faith does not deny that there is a final goal, does not say all is relative, but it does give legitimacy to the half truths and incomplete renderings that I find are characteristic of my faith life.

In these chapters, then, I want to explore some of the topics that are part of my own search for meaning and faith in my life.

Theological controversies over the centuries seem focused on the differences and an attempt to prove one position by vanquishing the other. People fought wars, figurative and literal, over issues like transubstantiation or consubstantiation, whether the Communion wafer was changed (trans) into a new substance, the body and blood of Jesus, or whether the wafer kept its characteristics of bread while also being (con) the body and blood of Jesus. At least I think that is the way the argument went. Nowadays I am pretty fuzzy on the exact differences and even less clear about what was at stake of the one over the other. There may be a number of readers out there going apoplectic at the moment over my rough skating over important issues. This book is not for them. Many other issues seem to me to be in this nether world of fuzzy faith: the Trinity, Jesus as fully God and human, the afterlife, to name just a few. During the chapters I will talk about some of these and how fuzzy faith operates for me.

Any areas in your faith that are fuzzy?

That's an area of theological doctrine that I am fuzzy about; there are other areas that are just as murky for me. Let's take one from the realm of religious practice: what about prayer? Or as the manuals would have it, the efficacy of prayer.

What do I believe about prayer and how it works and what its benefits are? All right, let's start with a confession, no, not that kind of confession, which would certainly be another hot topic. But here's my confession: Once a week I go to a local hospital to talk to patients and to give out Communion to those who wish. Now this is a great hospital in one of the most densely populated areas of Seattle. It has all of the modern amenities and technologies. Except parking. The parking garage is ancient and woefully inadequate for the volume of cars that attempt to park there each day. I usually arrive on the scene just after lunch, when the trolling for spaces is fiercest. I have a plan: I pray to St. Jude, St. Anthony of Padua, and Mary. Jude because he is the patron saint of hopeless causes, Anthony because he handles things that are lost, and Mary because she's Mary.

Now I know this is closer to superstition than prayer, but I also know it's been working for me. So what do I think of this? Do I think those three are sitting around upstairs searching out suitable spots for my Honda? Of course not. On the other hand, do I think the prayers are utterly worthless and meaningless? Well, no, I'm not ready to admit that either or I would have stopped doing them a while back.

So what's the solution? Which one's the answer? They can't both be right. Either that prayer is a naive child's game akin to Christmas wishes or saints are set up to man the phones at a heavenly help center. Which is it?

Before I answer that, let me cloud the issue more. I have spent most of my adult life teaching at high schools. Invariably, prayers will be offered up for the sports teams, a prayer for victory for our football team, say, as they sally forth to confront the monsters and behemoths incubated by the powerhouse school down the street. Do I think the prayers make our 150 pound linemen wipe out the 300-pounders across the line of scrimmage? Well, scores over the years bear out that the prayers don't trip the balance. But are the prayers then a waste of time? No, I say.

To take a more poignant case: the prayers of a family for

a parent or a child with cancer. What about those prayers? Do they have the power to alter the outcome? This is again a fuzzy area for me, where I am not ready to side with empiricists who point out the harsh realities of an inexorable, rampaging disease. I believe that prayer can in some way at times affect outcome and also change the individuals praying. How does that happen? I can't explain it, but I have faith that the prayer has very important positive parts to it.

Is God (or God's angels and saints) waiting and willing to intervene directly in human history to alter the natural chain of events? I'm thinking not usually, but God did it at least once, so no reason why it couldn't happen again. Even though probably not. Yet. . . I pray. And when a friend asks what it means to pray for the dead, I can't come up with a clear answer, but there is a fuzzy sense that praying for and to my parents, for example, is a good thing.

And I'm still getting a parking spot every week!

# 3 DICHOTOMY

Manicheanism is the belief that creation is made up of good and evil. Big deal! We know that, right? But with Manicheanism some things are good and some things are bad, evil. Ah, now we're into something quite different than a view that the world and all in it were once good, as viewed by God himself. Now we're into a situation where some things and people came into the world as already evil.

That's different. This is a world where our enemies aren't just wrong, they're born wrong, born evil. They are not like us, good people who see things differently, but people who from the beginning are not of God. They are DEMONS.

Demonizing those who oppose us solves all of the problems. We don't have to treat them fairly, listen to their side, try to understand them. And mostly we don't have to do the one thing that Jesus tells us to, the one thing that distinguishes Christian belief from other rational pursuits: We don't have to love them, a concept I will deal with in more detail in the "Big Deal" chapter later if you're still reading.

But to get to the point of this chapter, rigid faith leads to that dichotomy that brings judgment. There is something clean and appealing to a black/white view of life. We are saved or we're not, more importantly others are saved or not, because let's face it, we always see ourselves as in the saved group. When we read the stories about Jesus, we are standing with him. We see the hypocrites and Pharisees for what they are. In fact, we could give Jesus a number of modern equivalents, people today right in our own lives who are morally bankrupt.

They're all around us, but they're never us. What is the saying? We do something wrong because we make a mistake. We are good people who misstep. Others lie or cheat or steal because they are bad. We occasionally do bad things, but they are bad people. That's a perfect Manichean argument.

So, we're standing with Jesus and pointing out all of the bad people and sympathizing with him because it's hard to get even 12 good men (or women, although that might be easier) together. Just ask Noah, it's never been easy to find good people. So, we're standing there with Jesus, us good people, and we're helping him identify and condemn the bad, and frankly at times, although it's not good to say, but Jesus himself seems a little slow on the uptake, a little late at identifying the evil that we see so readily in others. It's easier for us, of course, because evil is just so clear in those who are against us. (He who isn't for me is against me.)

And this quick identification leads to one of my favorite images of God: God as our personal pit bull. Some day, maybe not today, God will give this person who I see as evil, what he or she so richly deserves. If not in this life, then certainly at the last judgment. They won't get away with it forever. That is the meaning of that terrible phrase: God is not fooled. You may think you're getting away with something, Miss High and Mighty, but just you wait. God will not be mocked. I know, because God and I are close, really close, in fact, God in this configuration is nothing more than an extension of my own beliefs and prejudices and petty hatreds. It's a small god indeed, but it's my god.

It was a great leap forward in my own faith to realize that God didn't particularly like me better than other people. That's not to say that there was no personal relationship with God, but rather that my relationship wasn't the only one God cared about. Much as I wanted to be, I wasn't the favored son. God loved me, yes, but God also loved all of his children with that same intense love.

In my youth I was tormented by the bully of the town,

we'll call him Marty Rayburn, although that was not his name. Luckily, Marty didn't go to my school, so I didn't have to contend with him often. But once in a while I would run into Marty and his gang, and he did always seem to travel with an entourage of sycophantic followers. I, alas, always seemed to be alone when I ran into him and suffered the consequences.

Marty was my version of the Philistines and I prayed as fervently as the Psalmist for my deliverance from his hands, but to no avail. The Psalmist not withstanding, God was not about to vanquish all my foes. He wasn't going to smash Marty's bloody carcass upon the rocks, he wasn't even going to trip him up a little and bloody his nose. In fact, it would appear that God loved Marty as much as he loved me. This was a hard concept to grasp. If God was omniscient, all-knowing, surely God could see all of the rotten things Marty did and represented. Surely justice demanded that God love me, who admittedly had some faults, but c'mon, I was a whole lot nicer kid than a sleaze-ball like Marty Rayburn. This was a no-brainer, God had to like me more, but for liking me more he was doing a lousy job of protecting me.

I had to face it at some point in my life: God did love me, but he also liked smelly bullies like Marty Rayburn. It was a disappointing realization in the short run, but a comforting insight in the long run to realize that God was a God of us all and not in it just to take care of me. The universalizing of God's care went a long way toward stretching the solipsism of my faith into a wider embrace. If I should ever get to the point of truly loving my enemies it will be because of this starting point.

The Jesus of the gospels calls to me; says,
Judge not, lest you be judged. I don't want to let
that out of my control, though.

# 4 HOT DOGS AND DOGMAS

The old adage warns us that there are two things that we should never watch how they are made. If we hope to keep liking them, don't scrutinize the making of laws and sausages. If this were an erudite tome ensconced high upon the New York Times best seller list, I would at this point lead you on a meticulous study of some law passed while I served in the U.S. Congress to prove the truth of that axiom. Alas, since this is a decidedly less scholarly work, I can only attest to the truth of the saying by recounting my experience one summer working in the hog kill of a large meat processing plant.

I won't, however, take you through that tour since it's been done countless times; I will just say that for many people, watching that tan effluvium oozing through a hose into the sausage casings would be enough to put one off his need to wolf down a couple of dogs at the next family picnic. But to be honest, after a few days the initial aversion to the sausage product abates and one's hunger for that All-American symbol returns just as heartily as my own appetite for meat returned bit by bit. By the end of my first week on the line where my job was to pull the pancreas out of the mass of hog guts floating by on the conveyer belt, I was quite ravenous come lunch time. And while I don't at this point in my life eat meat, it has less to do with the process and more to do with the look of the animals being herded into that narrow entrance that would seal their faith.

I would like to expand that list of laws and hot dogs by

adding dogmas, which I consider a type of laws. Dogmas would appear to be something unique to the Catholic tradition, and while they constitute only a portion of the faith of a Catholic they have in practice occupied a much larger space in our attention. Once I look at the history of the formulation of some dogmas I am carried back to my days at the meat packing plant. As we look at that process here, please note that I am in no way trying to pass myself off as an expert in the history of the Church, but again I am sauntering forth into that wilderness with as fragile a walking stick as I have. I would like to examine the evolution of dogmas and then talk about the significance of them in the life of faith.

Let's start with one that is surely foremost in the identity of the faith of a Roman Catholic: the belief in the infallibility of the pope. From the beginning people -- men and women -- followed Jesus. They listened to him, liked what he had to say, and wanted to imitate him in their own lives. And so, if they were fortunate enough to see Jesus firsthand, they threw down their fishing nets or their money changing equipment and they followed him. Later, they followed Jesus because the heard from the original followers, and so forth, on and on. At first, as the Acts of the Apostles tells us, they were a revolutionary little band, sharing their homes and their money and food.

But as time went by and numbers grew, more organization was called for, and as various accounts of who Jesus was were written, it became important to weed out the spurious from the genuine. And so the Church appointed men (alas) to function in various capacities, with the highest of these positions being bishops. Then as numbers grew and areas of the known world were reached with the gospel, the number of bishops increased, which in itself called for some sorting out of a hierarchy among bishops, someone to call the others together and keep order. Not someone better or more powerful, just someone in charge. Well, of course, you can see how long that would last. Invariably, those from more important areas saw their position as more influential. Jerusalem would be a logical place for the claim of primacy because of its importance in Jewish life and in the life of Jesus. The same also for Rome as the power of the Roman Empire waxed. So also for Constantinople after the rise of Constantine in the 300s. The same for places like Alexandria and a number of other cities, probably most of the major ones, although I don't think Milwaukee was in the mix.

Eventually, Rome and Constantinople emerged as the primary powers, and each made its claim that led to divisions that are still with us today. In the Western tradition, Rome's claim for supremacy and the backing of the bishop of Rome to be considered most important grew, but not without its opponents. As the centuries slid by, the claim of the Roman bishop morphed from the idea of first among equals to just plain first. Again, this claim was not without its detractors, which led to shoring up the claim of the legitimacy of the Roman bishop as the successor to Peter and the rightful head of the Church, an idea well suited to a world used to a triangle of power with a king at the top.

The dogma of the infallibility of the Pope is simply one more step along this process. It emphasizes that the Pope is guided by the Spirit and so leads the Church forward in infallible certainty into the future. Stated thus, it has an august ring to it. Understood in daily life, it took on a much more common aura. As children we understood more like a super power. Like if he wanted to, the Pope could tell us whether it was going to rain for the school picnic or in what year the Cubs would finally win the World Series. These were clearly not the intent of the dogma, but they were side effects.

Even when more judicious minds weighed in on the subject of infallibility, the results were not always so clear or illuminating. Papal infallibility, we were reminded was only in place when the Pope spoke about matters of faith and dogma. His thoughts and opinions on daily life and politics were as subject to error as any other person's. All good and well until you tried to distinguish between issues of faith and dogma and issues of importance but not matters of infallibility. Were pronouncements on the Trinity or the divinity of Jesus on the same level as teachings about contraception or artificial insemination? What came under the umbrella of infallibility and what was simply a matter of a very important leader of the Church speaking to his flock?

The dogma of papal infallibility, then, did not leap like Athena fully developed from day one; it evolved over the centuries like many of the other dogmas. The issue before us today is what kind of a role do these dogmas play in the life of faith. A few points seem clear. First, not many Catholics are sure of what is and is not a dogma, a matter of faith and morals that must be believed. There are many complex issues that popes address in encyclicals and through other means, and these are essential in our ongoing mission of understanding how to follow Jesus in a confusing world. Such discussions rely on thinking and praying and interpreting Jesus' life and message; they don't have anything to do with dependence on some variation on a voice from another dimension posing sphinx-like riddles for us.

Do we abandon such a belief then? That's probably not necessary any more than it is advantageous to go to war to protect it. It is truly one of those fuzzy issues where our time and energies would be better used pursuing other matters. The example of Pope Francis provides a striking illumination of what is important in this matter. Francis is less worried about receiving the proper respect due to him as pope and more concerned with finding ways of following Jesus more closely in modern life and using this faith to eradicate the problems facing us today. The respect comes without his having to make a case for its importance.

The issue of dogmas, then, muddies the scene and leads us away from an examination of the important issues to battle over symbols. Papal infallibility looms as one of those badges that separate Catholics from other Christian groups and emphasizes the divisions without leading to any fruitful meeting of believers. For example, the matter of papal infallibility switches emphasis from the Pope speaking the mind of the bishops and leading the faithful in a discernment of what is important and where the Spirit of Jesus is leading us in today's world.

# 5 ENOUGH

It's an old story. A husband and wife are shown around the estate of an extremely wealthy family. As the guide shows them the spacious grounds with tennis court and swimming pool, the wife leans in to her husband and whispers, "I know what they don't have." The guide, overhearing, leads them to the garage, where the Porsches and Land Rovers sit, but the wife repeats her comment, "I know what they don't have."

And so it goes throughout the tour. One wonderful room after another elicits the same response from the wife, "I know what they don't have." Until finally the guide explodes and challenges the wife, "What is it then that they don't have?"

"Enough," she responds.

We spend our lives chasing more so fiercely that we don't enjoy the now. Our view of what others have spoils the view of what we ourselves possess. Our present is occluded by the miasma of what might be. It's a nice house, but if we could live over there with a view of the water or the mountains. I like my job, but if I could get that promotion. I tell my students glibly that money doesn't buy happiness, and I truly believe that and have seen any number of examples of that in my own life. So why do I go out every so often and buy lottery tickets if I truly believe money doesn't buy happiness?

What is it that makes us want more than we have, to not be satisfied with what we possess? The very word satisfied contains the Latin word satis, which means "enough." A satisfied person knows she has enough. There is not a need to tear around and add to her empire; what she has is sufficient. She has enough.

The prayer here is one that you can use over and over. I do. It is for me less a prayer and more of a hope. I say, "I have enough."

"I have enough." I say, trying to convince my greedy self that I really do. In spite of being in the top 10% of people who have in the world, I spend my days thinking that I need more, that I don't have enough. In the meantime I don't half enjoy the things I already have.

Here's an exercise that for me is humbling: Go through your closet or your drawers. Pull out the things there you didn't even realize you had. I can find shirts or a sweater or a pair of pants that I haven't worn in forever, probably something that I'm on the verge of buying a new one just like it, simply because I have more things than I realize. And this in spite of periodic forays on the closet and clothes drawers to take things to St. Vincent de Paul or Goodwill.

"I have enough" is one of the most powerful prayers I have ever encountered. It is a sharp rebuke to that greedy side of my nature, that pack-rat within me that wants to store things against a rainy day.

And I have no history to justify this insecurity. I have never been without to such an extent that I can say I need to do this. I remember being with some of my relatives at a lunch one time. We had gone to a restaurant after a funeral, about 10 or 12 of us at some informal place like a Denny's or Cracker Barrel. As we left, I put a little extra money on the table because I knew the tip was light and I always liked to tip a lot since I had spent years dependent on tips myself.

My uncle, a truly wonderful generous man, saw me doing that and he said to me. "You know, I can never do that. I grew up during the Depression and we didn't have anything and so I always think that what I have might disappear at any moment and so I just can't bring myself to do that."

I understood what he was saying, but of course that hadn't been my experience at all. There was never a time where we were destitute. We could have had more, and I was constantly aware of how much I didn't have, but in truth we had more than enough to survive. And yet, it was not enough for me. And so I pray, "I have enough." To remind myself that I do and to quiet the junkyard dogs of greed that tell me I need more.

"I have enough." It is a prayer tied to happiness and living in the moment more than almost any other I can think of.

Say it now. I have enough. Do you believe it? Say it five times, and as you do, think of all of the ways you do have enough. Think of the many material and psychological and spiritual gifts you have. Open those closets and drawers of your life and gaze upon the many possessions you have. I have enough. Think of all the things you haven't thought about or been thankful for in a long time. Think how important they are next to the bauble in front of you that you think you can't live without.

I have enough. Say it, pray it, until you believe it.

This concept of enough, though, doesn't just apply to objects; it is equally applicable to talents. We frequently think of ourselves as not having as much ability as others, and this can block our attempts to do the Lord's work. We read about great women and men doing great things and we dismiss this by saying we don't have those abilities to do the work of a Mother Teresa. We are like Moses telling God he can't really lead his people because he stutters. Any port in a storm! Any excuse that will get us out of work, we use it. I can't do that, I don't have that kind of determination or that kind of vision or that much intelligence. That's great for those who do, but I'll just sit back and lead the quiet life. After all, if God wanted that out of me, he would have given me more ability, better skills. I'm not really cut out for that sort of work.

I don't have enough talent. I don't have enough charisma, leadership ability, organizational skills, you fill in the blank of what keeps you from attempting something beyond what you have done, something that God may be calling you to do, but you find yourself unfit for the challenge, because you don't have enough.

How often do we celebrate our own talents without comparison to others? Do we prize our own intellect without looking at it in contrast to someone else who we think is smarter, wiser, more perceptive? Are we able to look at our own athletic ability and be happy with that without comparing it to another person's? Our artistic taste? Our poise or grace? It's an unfortunate by-product of television and other media that we are constantly exposed to the accomplishments and abilities of the very best in every field, so that we can't prize our own talents without seeing out-size illustrations of other people excelling in those same areas. Consequently, we discount our own talents and perhaps fail to use the gifts God gave us. Can a child jump, run, shoot a basketball any more without comparing himself to Michael Jordan or Stephan Curry? When he can, he gives himself up to the joy and glory of the game itself and relishes his own flashes of expertise. When he can't, he is never satisfied with his effort which falls short of what others accomplish. Again, he doesn't have enough. Enough possessions, enough talent.

Enough time. Another aspect where we immobilize ourselves by saying we don't have enough of it to do the things we would like. If we had more time, we would take the kids to Disneyland. But we don't. Although we do have enough time to take them across the street to a park where we could fly a kite or kick a ball around. We don't have enough time to go away for a 30-day retreat. But we do have enough time to pray for 15 minutes in the evening. We don't have enough time to travel to a distant country to work with the poor. But we would have the time to teach one person how to read. The list of things we don't have time for obscures the many things we do have time for.

Say it again: I do have enough time. I have enough time to do the Lord's bidding. One of my favorite quotes, I think it's from the Psalms (or Isaiah): "Seek the Lord while he may be found." We have enough time to find the Lord. But that is a time-sensitive treasure. The Lord may only be found while we have the time. He is not there forever. Seek him, now, while he may be found. We have enough time. And then we don't.

The line from the Psalms provides an imperative along

with a warning. Seek the Lord now in all ways, but know that your time is limited. At your back time's winged chariot is hurrying near. It is the Kairos, the time of Grace that is there at one point on the continuum and then is gone. It is the Christian analogue of Carpe diem, but here there is none of the sybarite's garnering all the pleasure he can. Here the time is short, so seek God in all of his creation now while he may be found. You don't have much time, so do His will now.

You put off helping a friend or working at a soup kitchen or reconciling a past quarrel. There's always tomorrow, you reason. But there isn't. Your time is sand running out of the glass, and while you have it, Seek the Lord. Now, while he may be found. For one day he will no longer be found, one day you will no longer be able to feed his poor, comfort his sad ones, house his wandering lost souls. There is only now, the psalmist warns us, do it now while you can. Seek the Lord while he may be found. Seek him now in this Advent season! the saying is a great existential corrective to our extemporizing.

Something ingrained in our culture makes the feeling of being happy with what we have seem inadequate. It goes against our acquisitive spirit to say we have enough. It seems passive, settling for, instead of looking to grow and increase. But being content with what we have is not a passive thing. It takes a great active effort of governing our desires and urges to always add something more to our domain. Our desire to hunker down and hoard is much more powerful than our need to give or share from our wealth. "It is mine, I've earned it." Is the cry of pride that drowns out the humble thought that all we have is gift and so all we have is to be shared with others. That fundamental insight, though, of having been given so much by God nourishes the response of wanting to reach out and share. It is the action of a strong person to reach out from her secure spot and pull someone else up onto the life raft.

From this underlying realization of God's great love of me, I can truly make mine the prayer of St. Ignatius for generosity:

Take Lord, and receive all my liberty, my memory, my
understanding, and my entire will, all that I have and possess.
Thou hast given all to me. To Thee, O lord, I return it. All is
Thine, dispose of it wholly according to Thy will. Give me
Thy love and thy grace, for this is sufficient for me.

# 6 ENVY

When I think of myself in my worse light I have this image: I am waiting in a line. I hate lines and waiting. My wife thinks it's because I have no patience, but that's not really the answer; the explanation lies in a deeper, more primitive reaction: I'm afraid they'll run out. One place I taught gave the teachers free lunch once a week. Everyone would line up, as did I. While I waited for my turn, there was the underlying fear, they're not going to have enough, I'm not going to end up with anything, all of the good things will be gone, all that will be left will be root vegetables.

In spite of the fact that they would rarely run out and that I'm vegetarian and kind of like root vegetables, there remains that primal fear that there won't be enough. Maybe it has to do with survival of the fittest and one's own survival, but for me it is tied into a theological vision from my youth. I see a long line of souls waiting to enter heaven and the fear is that I won't make it, they will close the gates before I get in. No stadium seating for me! That image of being left out in the cold is hard to shake.

What does this have to do with envy? The fear of not being served at some point makes us incapable of enjoying what we have in the same way that our envy of the things others have forces our view away from our blessings and onto what we don't have that others do.

A telling moment when you go out to eat is when the waiter brings the courses out for everyone at the table. For some their eyes are on their own, looking at it, telling if it's what they ordered and whether it was prepared right. Some people though are constantly flitting from theirs to the other dinners, judging whether theirs is as big or good as the others. I knew a man who never enjoyed a meal out in his life because he was always thinking I should have ordered what she got or why did I only get two small pieces of fish and he got three big ones? The envy overwhelmed any contentment the meal should bring.

The antidote for envy, according to the mystics, is radical. Radical? It's absurd in its full iteration. There are many mystics we can turn to for an explanation of this, but I will use St. Ignatius because he always seemed to have a way of putting the most esoteric and ethereal into practical, dollars and cents sense. Ignatius said that the cure for envy is to go to the other extreme: to wish for the worst. Not even that it was ok to get something bad or substandard, but to actually wish for it. I told you it was absurd, but he gets worse.

So, in the simple example of the diner, he would not only accept the poorer portion, but he would actively seek it. If there were one bad dinner among the twelve dinners, he would wish to get it.

Marvelous! See how that obliterates envy? You now waste no time worrying about receiving the worst, because you actually want it. You don't have to check around to compare, because you already are happy with the worst

Even more radically, it solves my basic fear of being rejected from Heaven. Many saints, but I'm thinking at the moment of St. Teresa of Avila, expressed such deep faith that they didn't even fear the loss of heaven. Teresa said that if it would lessen the suffering of Jesus in his passion she would gladly suffer the pains of hell. And this from a woman who passionately believed in the reality of heaven and hell, of salvation and damnation.

Ignatius called this concept Indifference. Indifference meant to Ignatius that it didn't matter what came -- the best, the worst, riches, poverty, sickness, health, etc. -- he was fine as long as he was doing the will of the Father.

What a great antidote to the anxiety of worrying about

getting our share! We can't be hurt by what we get or don't get, because our happiness is not dependent upon that. We may strive for and want something, but if we don't get it, that is all right as long as we feel we are living and working and being what we truly should be. If I could just acquire that trait, I would be eternally happy. Nothing would bother me, I wouldn't be sitting around wishing for anything. I'm really envious of those people with true indifference. I wish I had it. Oh, wait a minute. Oh, I guess . . .

# 7 FENCE THEORY

I'm terrible at a party. People think I'm an extrovert and must love parties, but in truth I hate that feeling of vulnerability of striking up a conversation with a stranger. Then things get even worse if that person comes up with a question like what sort of animal would you like to be. At that point I freshen up my drink or take up drinking if I haven't already.

With that in mind, I ask you this annoying psychological parlor game question: What kind of fence are you?

Not only annoying, but stupid! But the difference is that it's my annoying question and therefore I like it. The question rests on the theory, shared by me and no one else that I can think of, that all of humanity can be classified by the type of fence they represent. For example, I think of myself as a cyclone fence, do you know the type? It's a steel fence with braided wire forming holes about two inches wide in a diamond pattern. They're frequently around construction sites, etc.

Let me explain my theory if you haven't already skipped this chapter. I was given a book that I read even though it violated a deathbed promise I had made to my mother never to read a book with a unicorn on the cover. In spite of this infelicitous choice which the author may not have had any part in, the book was very perceptive about the human soul, which is to say that he put into words ideas similar to my own experience. The author, Michael A. Singer, maintains that the key to life is being able to identify the center of our consciousness, our spirit or soul, and to allow it to merely see experiences and let them pass through as part of life. Good and bad experiences, the key is to view them with equanimity and allow them to pass through, without trying to hang onto them. I think a visual for this idea is to see the self as a type of fence. If you are a solid wood or metal fence, nothing gets through. Old shopping bags, candy wrappers, french fry boxes, every bit of trash piles up against your impervious wall. If you're a little more open, like a screen, some things, like air and a few tiny bits, could flow through, maybe an occasional gnat. A larger, airier fence, like a cyclone, would let some papers and debris sail through. A really spacey fence with no wire would let everything through, and that would be ideal, since your spirit would hold onto nothing from the past and would meet each new experience unencumbered by the flotsam and jetsam of the the past.

To drop the metaphor for the moment, which is hard for me since I like it so much: when we hang onto past animosities it is difficult to meet new people without some of the bitterness that characterizes those past experiences -- or to meet the person who was the source of those feelings again. If I have been burned in the past when I tried to share my feelings, it is hard for me not to hang onto that experience and let it color whether I take risks sharing my feelings in the future. If I get divorced, it is hard to enter into another loving relationship with the optimism and hope I brought to the first one. That is because the trash of the first relationship has blown up against my narrow fence (see, I couldn't stay away from the metaphor long!) and blocked the passage of the wind through it.

It works the same for good experiences. If I try to hold onto those experiences, I cause just as much a blockage. The wonderful experiences of Christmas at my family's house when I was young makes it hard to go to my wife's family for Christmas. I will always be comparing it unfavorably to my family's experience. The good friends I made one place preclude my making new friends when I am forced to move to another town. There's too much garbage that has blown up against my fence.

It's a useful way to look at life, I think. We experience hundreds of things and people each day of our lives. Many pass through without a noticeable effect on us, but others shape and color our perspective on everything else. How else to explain something like racial prejudice, but that someone or something conditioned us to view persons of a different racial group as threatening or hostile or in some way not like us? Once formed, we carry these perspectives forward until someone or something challenges us to relinquish them.

People are all kinds of fences. Some are closely fitted wood fences that let almost nothing through. It takes a hurricane to get anything through those fences. There is a story about a politician who was riding in a convertible down Main Street after winning the election. He could point to every store along the way and tell you whether the owner had allowed him to put up a campaign sign in the window. This was a person who had a tight fence. Another person could never meet someone new without already putting that person into one of the categories (mostly negative)of people he had had problems with. There was no way for him to be surprised by a new discovery because he was already he had cataloged what this new person was like.

Most of us are not quite that closed off, but we do have some blockage there that keeps us from letting all of the past flow through unimpeded. I said that I see myself as a cyclone fence; what about you? What kind of fence are you? Take a moment to decide now what kind of fence you are? How much blockage is there in your life?

The same holds true for those defenses that we hang onto. My own cynical, sarcastic exterior that holds a new person at a distance comes from a lifetime of experience, it is a Cheetos bag blown up against my cyclone fence that I cannot let go of. I continue to let such debris gather. Perhaps at one point I appeared too naive, too indiscriminately trusting and was wounded in that vulnerable area by some offhand remark, and I vowed to cover up so that it didn't happen again. I was clever enough to shield myself from being hurt again. That is wisdom in the worldly manner. But what if I chose to let go of that hurt, to not be changed by it, to approach my next meeting with a new person in the same trusting way I had used before? What if I simply let go of the earlier experience? The holes in my fence would widen and I would no longer be governed by what happened to me in the past.

In my home I have a banner that reads:
In the end what matters most is
How well did you live?
How well did you love?
How well did you learn to let go?

It is that last line that is difficult for me, to truly let go of things and people and to live in the moment facing what and who is there for me. If I am able to widen the holes of my fence, I can let more and more simply pass through without trying to latch onto each thing. The great saints, I think, didn't have any fence at all left by the end of their lives. St. Ignatius, for example, could make his prayer that most ridiculous of statements that he was totally indifferent to what God did to him because it all just brought him closer to the Lord. I will talk more about this indifference at the end of this book, but a clear insight can be gained right now by seeing that the fenceless saint holds onto nothing, desires nothing, because her soul is already in perfect peace. She needs no more. She does not say, If I just conquer this fault or cultivate this virtue, I will be perfect and one with the Lord and at peace.She does not even say, If I read just one more book on spirituality I know that I can become truly holy. No, she perceives that as she widens her fence and allows all of these events of her life to pass through without trying to control them or defend against them, she will be content and at peace.

So what kind of fence are you? Is yours open enough to let go of the past or do you hang onto it and make it impossible to meet the Lord in the new experiences ahead of you?

You might try that now. What is the trash of life blowing up against your fence? What has gotten caught so that you can't simply be? So that you can't just know that you are perfectly in the embrace of God at this very moment. Can you let go of all that debris? Identify it, let it pass through, and simply watch it blow away leaving you in peace and harmony with all of life. Can you do that? If so, you can close this book up and just go out and watch the river flow!

# 8 PRAYER

There were periods in my life where I spent a good part of the day in prayer: an hour in the morning, Mass, prayer at lunch, a half hour in the afternoon, and then again some time before retiring at night.

It was good.

It was also something that I could not sustain for the rest of my life. At the time I was in a religious order where such a regimen could be fit into my daily schedule, but that was not something that I could continue to practice for the rest of my life. In time the prayer periods became shorter and less frequent. At times, a half hour period seemed like something that I could do all the time, but I found over the years that I was not faithful to that either.

Of late, under the direction of a very savvy guru, I have aimed at 15 minutes of prayer each day, and I have been fairly faithful to that. However, I am astounded that I can easily go a whole day without taking out that amount of time to pray. What does that mean? Am I that weak and inconsistent in my faith? Well, yes, but that's not the whole answer.

And what about Jesus' injunction to pray unceasingly, to pray always? What are we to make of that? Here's my solution.

Finding a block of time is great. I have spent my whole life trying to do that with medium success. When I do it, I'm happy and when I fail to do it, I'm guilty. I'm not sure that is the outcome God wants. Anyway, finding a block of time is a nice solution for you if it works. For those who don't have success with that, I propose this. Just a short prayer. Nothing long. Fifteen seconds in duration, maybe, but simply a brief turning of your mind to God.

Years ago these little prayers went by the unfortunate name of ejaculations, a title taken over by other areas of human endeavor and may hint at why they fell out of favor. More than one pure-minded nun was perplexed by the reaction when she advocated that fifth-grade boys should try for more ejaculations each day. The poorly suppressed laughter of the boys led inexorably to the gradual erosion of the use of term in theological discussions.

Which is too bad, since the practice is a very good one that would be a great help in one's spirituality today.

The use of these short prayers has a deep root in the history of our spirituality. Russian monks taught the Jesus Prayer to the Russian peasants. These simple, illiterate souls had no great theological training and no ability to sit down and read esoteric tracts on the nature of God and prayer. They required instead easy, vivid phrases to reinforce their belief and to serve as an act of presence before God. The Jesus Prayer was perfect. A modern English rendition runs like this: "Lord Jesus Christ, Son of the living God, have mercy on me a sinner." The phrase, repeated over and over, assumes the rhythm of our own breathing until it is so second nature that the person is literally praying always, unceasingly, much like a mantra in other beliefs. It takes no theological training and no special intelligence to say them, in fact knowledge and intellect get in the way of these powerful simple phrases.

The prayer can be any phrase. I have found over the years that I fall back on the Hail Mary, for whatever reason, but it can be any phrase of any length. One that I have developed over the years reins in my sometimes galloping anxiety and centers me here in the moment, which is at the heart of most spiritualities that I have seen. It is a very simple three-block prayer:

This is it.
Right now.
Right here.

The key phrase is This is it. It's a simple yet powerful acknowledgment that what you are experiencing this moment right here is the center of life. This is all we have, not something coming in the future, not some other place we hope to get to, but right now and right here is our only true reality. Until we come to the point where we acknowledge that and accept it, we will not be truly happy.

We cannot think that I will do that once I get this project done or once this period is over, I will be happy or I will pray or I will find God in my life. Right here, right now. That is the essence of happiness. It's the heart of meditation which tries to focus our thoughts and consciousness in the present. Through a concentration of effort on, for example, our breathing, we are able to be fully present in the present.

Again the story from the past: Some saint, I don't remember which one if indeed it was told about only one saint, but the story goes like this. A group of monks were asked what they would do if they were told they had only one hour left to live. The first monk replied that he would run to his confessor and be pardoned for all of his sins in his life. The second declared that he would seek forgiveness from anyone he had offended. Another said he would spend the time remaining in prayer, and so it went down the line until finally the last monk said simply, "I would continue weeding the garden as I had been doing." The moral being that the work set before us, the world we are in is where our salvation is forged.

We may indeed dream of doing great and miraculous things, but in the meantime we let the moments of salvation slip away, unaware that we find God right in front of us in the people and tasks we have near at hand. The reality of the moment never seems as appealing as the possibility of the future. One day we will do great things; at the moment we wait and let the moments of grace slip through our fingers like Miniver Cheevy, the subject of the E. A. Robinson poem, who dreams of doing great deeds in the era of knights in armor, but misses out on life happening all around him.

This is it. This is life. Right now, right here. It's our life, the one given us by God and we need to live it as fully and consciously as possible.

That is the prayer. This is it, right here, right now.

But regardless of the content, the central insight of this method is that it emphasizes frequency over length. It involves turning your mind to God often during the day rather than once or twice for a longer period of time. Turning your mind toward God twenty times a day is, I think, preferable to spending a longer period in prayer and then not thinking of God the rest of the day. It is a form of obeying Jesus' advice to pray unceasingly. It is also in the spirit of St. Ignatius' examen, where the emphasis is on turning to the Lord at various key moments in our day.

So to practice this, try to say one short prayer a number of times during the day. Perhaps it is something like, "Jesus, teach me patience today." Or "Lord, let me be content with what I have." Or "I love you, Lord Jesus." Anything works. It's not what is said, after all, God is not sitting around waiting for deep insights from us, prayer isn't about what we have to tell God, but rather the practice of turning toward him in love and attention. It is the acknowledgment of our creaturely relationship to God.

The point of this practice is simply to put ourselves in the presence of God. If we are able to do that, God will do the rest. We don't and can't wrestle like Jacob and the angel into making God submit to our efforts. We would rather wait upon God knowing that is sufficient. Sometimes we get the idea that true, meaningful prayer must consist of deep thoughts we share with God or that God infuses into our hearts and minds. Afterwords, we can share these pious, profound insights with our families and friends -- maybe even write a book about them!

But that is not the purpose of prayer. It is not some spiritual equivalent of going to the gym and working out. We don't really make progress in prayer like adding spiritual muscle mass. We don't really "get better" at prayer in the usual sense of increasing our mastery of some technique, like say improving our dexterity on the parallel bars. We can't hang a chart on the wall and plot our progress as we like to do with so many of our programs and activities. We can't say that we have progressed from Novice to Intermediate to Saint.

Prayer isn't an activity to master; rather, it is a relationship to foster and grow in. It has its periods of getting closer and being simpatico where everything comes easily and freely, and then it has its colder, drier periods where every word, every gesture seems strained and forced. In the process of this give and take we do indeed grow closer to the other person, but it's not a progress that we chart or check the level of.

No, we can spend many years praying and from a human standpoint make apparently no progress. I am amazed that after as many years as I have put in trying to pray to find how hard it is. I would never admit this to anyone other than you that I frequently feel like I am in prison putting in the time. I sometimes feel like Bart Simpson being stuck in school waiting for the 3:00 bell to ring while the hands moved slowly toward that 3:00 like approaching an asymptotic goal, getting closer and closer, but never quite reaching. So my prayer goes at times. I would be embarrassed if someone could peek inside my head and see how conscious of the clock I am like a weary assembly line worker.

I am comforted by two things. First, some of the greatest prayers, if I can use such a ridiculous term, struggled mightily with prayer. Theresa of Avila and John of the Cross, big time mystics, spent years without any discernible progress or consolation in their prayer. God rewarded two of his most faithful servants no favors or comforts in spite of their faithfulness and perseverance. As the saying goes, "If God treats his friends this way, no wonder he has so few."

The other thought is a favorite saying of George Winzenburg, a Jesuit who has spent many years on the Red Cloud Reservation in South Dakota. The saying didn't originate with George, I am sure, but I hear him saying it often in his soothing voice: Trying to pray is praying. Over the years that insight has brought great comfort to me. This is much the same insight that I have heard in other areas of life. A very patient yoga instructor, Nancy Siewert, once explained that the problem with yoga classes was that it gave people the opportunity to compare their progress against other people's, a very unyogic idea, since each person's progress is unique. One person's ability to contort into a pretzel might not be more beneficial than another's efforts to reach halfway to her toes. Each person's efforts is uniquely her own and not measurable against a standardized bell curve of excellence. In the same way, a heavy person's walk might bring him more benefit than a 5-mile run by a fit individual.

The lesson is clear: Prayer is a relationship that grows and develops according to dynamics of the two persons involved (in this case you and God), not a program that is geared toward spiritual proficiency. Take a moment to think about your prayer in a new way. What is the style of your relationship to God in prayer? Who are you? How do you talk to God when you pray? You build a style and a vocabulary of a relationship with God. What is yours? What do I mean by that? Here's an example. When I'm anxious and worrying about something, I tend to repeat a word or phrase over and over. I will say, "My Lord, my Lord, my Lord." Over and over, faster and faster, timing it almost with my heart beat racing, until I find myself running out of energy and slowing down and becoming calmer. Or I will say that Russian peasant prayer, "My Lord and my God, Son of the living God, have mercy on me a sinner." Over and over until I calm down into a slow, peaceful rhythm. Or the Hail Mary again and again, taking my focus away from my fear and centering it on Jesus.

In each of those, though, I am the fearful creature seeking solace. At other times my prayer is more peaceful and I just have fewer words and more attitude of thankfulness and peace. My vocabulary seems less important and shrinks to just a few words. I am not seeking anything, I'm just there.

At other times I'm too important to pray. I have too much going on. I'm watching the clock. Then I try for that sense of humor. I admit the absurdity of me being too busy for God. I try to make God laugh a little bit. I figure if I can do that, he might forget what a pompous, self-important little worm I can be.

What is your position with God? What are the words you use? What emotion predominates when You pray? Over the years you have built a style of praying, even if it's usually just pushing away or making excuses for not praying more. Whatever it is, it is your style and it's where you should begin when you pray to God, just by acknowledging what it is.

A final note about prayer, and I don't know where I came across this idea, I'm sure it's not mine originally, but the idea is to imagine that you have just 7 (don't know why that number) minutes left to live. What would you say to God then? What would be on your mind? It's an interesting idea, I think.

# 9 DARK NIGHT

St. Teresa of Avila and St. John of the Cross, probably the two most prominent symbols of fierce relationships with God, were both beset by years of spiritual aridity, wandering endlessly in an emotional desert without any solace or any encouragement to continue on. To read any of the literature about these two passionate saints is to bear witness to a tempestuous relationship with God that tested the extreme boundaries of faith and despair. Both endured emotions and disappointments that go far beyond the pallid faith lives of most of us. And yet, as they stood at the rim of despair and peered over into the abyss day by day, year by year, they clung to their faith and reaffirmed their belief in a God who had apparently turned his back on them for no discernible reason.

These two saints are extreme examples, but most of the saints recount similar experiences, although not generally of such long duration. The modern saint Mother Teresa, who we would think had to have enjoyed a splendid symbiotic relationship with God who would nourish her during her years of energetic work with the poor, instead spent long periods of aridity and darkness, faithfully praying without any encouraging signs from God. She forged ahead totally on the strength of her faith.

In your own life you have perhaps experienced some of this same dark night, but it is important to distinguish that passionate, turbulent dark night that the saints experienced from the mere absence that we sometimes feel because of our own lack of seeking the Lord while he may be found. There is a lassitude that assumes that since God is always there, he can wait until we're ready. Wait until the shopping is done, the game is over, the work is finished. This kind of inertia blocks us from experiencing God's presence, but it has nothing to do with the separation referred to by the dark night, which occurs in spite of the best efforts of those seeking the presence of the Lord.

I find that there is a big difference between when I diligently seek the Lord's presence and that passivity that lets me assume God's presence without ever consciously adverting to it.

My childhood now seems rife with stories of people (generally Communist atheists) who were trying to disabuse me of my faith. One of the standard ploys was to tell the believer to ask for something, and then when the requested item didn't come about, there was the proof that there was no God. Well, that didn't prove there was no God, it simply demonstrated that God wasn't a fairy-tale genie who was at the owner's beck and call (I always wanted to write a mystery novel about a team of detectives named Beck and Call). It just showed that God was beyond doing tricks like a trained monkey just to entertain the masses. In the same way, Jesus refused to work miracles merely because the crowds following him were looking for these signs.

God's timetable and to-do list, then, in no way coincides with our own. As the Psalmist says, God's ways are not our ways. God does come to answer Job when Job demands it, but only in his own time and manner. And even then, the answer is nothing like the yes/no definitiveness of a questionnaire completer. God answers, but Job is as confused as ever. He believes, but he's still confused. And that's when God answers. What about the missionaries in Silence or the great mystics, where God seemed to remain uncommunicative and remote?

Dark night is like any relationship: the hard times tend to define it. How a couple responds, for example, to the loss of a child determines their relationship. The tragedy pulls them closer together or it becomes a wedge of recrimination that drives them apart. So it is with God. The pain of no connection forces a terrible decision on the person. No more vividly is this illustrated than in the novel <u>Silence</u> by Shusaku Endo, which was later made into a powerful movie. Here the Jesuit missionaries sent to Japan in the 1600s endure many hardships, but all of these pale in comparison to the silence and apparent indifference of the God they worship. Crying for some sign of God's love, the central character is met with stony silence. This is the dark night that many saints have talked about, and the effects of it are devastating in this account. What human can be expected to persevere under such circumstance? The earlier missionary who has recanted his faith is seen first as weak, but later the struggle makes our judgments irrelevant.

Who can withstand such a desert of emotion and encouragement? The axiom of God never sending us more than we can endure seems woefully inadequate to explain this painful dilemma suffered by the Portuguese missionaries. And yet the silence they confront is the same that saints like John of the Cross or Theresa of Avila endured during their lifetimes. These figures stand not as condemnation of the lives of people like the missionaries in <u>Silence,</u> but as ideals of the capacity for love that can be found in humans at times, of the faith that can triumph over all reasonable ideas of limits and expectations. They are the models of what can be endured and accomplished, but thankfully not all of us will be called upon to meet such challenges.

# 10 STREET PEOPLE

I work sometimes in a homeless mission. We don't have the space to provide overnight shelter, but we are able to provide clothing, sleeping bags when we have them, a little food and coffee to help these people through the day. One of the rooms is the men's clothing section, and here I help men find suitable attire to replace what they have. One of the things that you don't expect unless you stop for a moment and think about it, is that most of the men are pretty fussy. In spite of your expectations, they won't take just any old thing, put it on and be satisfied with it. After a short time, I came to understand their feelings. In a rough life this was one of the few areas where they had any choice, any say over their lives and the circumstances they were in, so if they were offered a pink backpack, even though they really needed one, no thank you, I don't want pink.

A woman who worked with me one day failed to understand this process. Her attitude was, Hey, I was raised in a large family and I got hand me downs and I was glad to get them. If I didn't want them, I could just go without. So, you in your situation should be darned happy to get anything at all, so take it and be grateful and I don't want to hear any complaining. And of course I understood her reasoning, but it didn't at all speak to the men or what they were going through or how they saw things. For them, what little dignity they had left was tied up in being able to choose something in life, even if it was as small an item as which jacket they were going to wear or what was on the t-shirt they were putting on.

I think of that a lot as I pass homeless people on my way

somewhere. In Seattle most of the entrance and exit ramps of I-5 are manned by people with tattered cardboard signs asking for contributions. There are enough of these homeless there and on the busier street corners of Seattle that you cannot be oblivious to the exploding population of people without jobs or homes, and the tendency is to get worn out, to hit the saturation point where you say "Enough! I'm tired of seeing all of these people. Isn't there somewhere we can put them?" But the situation isn't being resolved, in fact it is growing worse, as most of us can see. What can be our response to it?

I am personally in a bind when I pass by these people asking for money. On the one hand I want to give and yet at the same time I have the nagging suspicions: Is he really homeless or just scamming me? How do I know that he isn't just collecting money to take his buddies drinking at the end of the day? I am caught in that classic lose-lose situation. If I pass him by, I feel guilty because I know I wouldn't miss a dollar or two that I might give him. If I give him a bit of money, I go away thinking I've been conned, that I just wasted my money that would be better spent if I gave it to a legitimate charity. That's why I love what Pope Francis had to say. When in doubt, just give. It's always better. Confronted with the double bind I mentioned above it's better to err, as Ignatius would say, on the side of charity. If you're going to make a mistake, let it be where you helped the person out.

I like that. I would rather be the chump than end up being so shrewd that I let someone starve or go without shelter. I recognize that these actions are not huge society-changing decisions. Whether I give or not does not impact the underlying causes of poverty and does nothing to eradicate it, but it is a step in a direction I would rather go.

In the classic story the little boy is walking along the beach with his mother. As he goes, the little boy stops at various points to toss one of the starfish littering the beach back into the sea. His mother, annoyed at the constant delays, admonishes him that he might as well give it up since he can't save them all. To which the boy responds, "No, but I can save these." My response in terms of the homeless probably isn't even no, but I can save this one, it's probably only, no, but at least I didn't stomp on the starfish.

Sometimes I let the enormity of a problem paralyze me. I see so much to be done that I despair of doing anything. That is a real lack of faith on my part, not only in God, but in myself and the gifts God has given me. I tend to trivialize my actions, to see those first few tentative steps toward a solution as so pitifully inadequate that I give up. I don't see the eventual solution, just the enormity of the problem and leave dejectedly. We tend to see the great accomplishments of the saints and think that we can never accomplish such great feats. We don't see the mistakes and timid first steps that these saints often took before they reached their goals.

# 11 REPETITION

Repetition plays a big role in faith. It is one of the things that alienates young people from the faith, and yet it is the same thing that brings us back to the faith later in life. There must be something about repetition that only appeals to a certain period in one's life. I remember being bored by the Mass when I was young (I don't claim to be beyond that even now in my dotage), but now it is some of that repetition that makes me bond with the ritual.

There are numerous elements of repetition in our faith. The Rosary is a series of those same prayers repeated over and over again until they become mumbled strands that are barely within the radar of our consciousness. At times the words tumble out almost without your knowledge. The Hail Marys flow one after the other while you occupy your mind with something altogether different.

At the Mass, if we go regularly, we hear the same gospel stories over and over. If we're careful, we may never hear anything new since we automatically shut down saying oh, I know that story about the Prodigal Son, I don't have to listen. But the familiar can also lead us to a comfortable bonding with the truths of the experience. Settling into the story of the prodigal son, we can let the lessons of the parable wash over our minds like water over the rocks slowly smoothing them to a new shape. We hear the story over and over until some new insight slides into our ken or we relish some old one in a new way. Or, as we age, we find we identify with a new character. The son no longer draws our attention as he did when we were twenty; now the father seems much more interesting to us.

But it is the repetition that anchors us to our faith. Even the church calendar, with its regular seasons of Lent and Advent give us a cyclic pattern that lends harmony and structure to our daily lives. My absolute favorite title "Ordinary Time" sums it up best. What nonentity cleric entombed in the caverns of the Vatican came up with that absolutely perfect name for a time of the year and of our lives? What time is it? It's Ordinary Time? Is it Easter, nope, not for a while. Christmas? Not even close. We're not even in the area of preparing for those. It's Ordinary Time. You know, that time of the year that we spend most of our lives at, the time when nothing special is going on, we're just here living through Ordinary Time. With its ups and downs, its cyclic magic, we either enjoy or despise the regularity, and in that simple decision we find our lives lovely or unrewarding.

The ultimate prayer of repetition, at least for those of us who don't belong to a monastic order, is the Rosary, a practice that I have had and lost and seem to have regained again later in my life. The Rosary, with its progression of Our Fathers, Hail Marys, and Glory Bes, seems to use the hypnotic repetition of the succession of prayers to put our minds into an attitude of receptivity to the Lord. The mechanics of the prayer, especially aided by a rosary, are not demanding so that our minds are free to wander along the lines of the mysteries of faith. In the progression our cares and fears come and go, appear and vanish while we slip back into the peaceful embrace of the familiar and the comforting embrace of God's love.

It seems that most spiritualities have practices that use the healing rhythm of repetition, perhaps because it excuses our mind from having to do a lot of work and allows the spirit to take over. In the Rosary the mechanical recedes into the background while the spirit predominates, the very attitude Mary must have had from the start when she was confronted with her most surprising challenge in life.

Repetition, then, celebrates that wide swath in our lives that our modern culture does not value: the lacunae between major events, those times where we're waiting for life to happen, but which in retrospect are the occasions where the moiety of life transpires. We work out our salvation in those quotidian moments of humdrum reality, just as we express our love in a marriage most fully not in those Precious Moments, but in the daily routine of doing little thoughtful favors or fulfilling implicit obligations or simply by being there when the other needs us.

Like the world, the repetition of our faith life goes on and on and on.

# 12 TRUST

I am by nature or nurture a cynical person. I have always wanted to be the meek and mild lamb of Jesus' parables and William Blake's <u>Songs of Innocence</u>, but I find myself more inclined toward the <u>Songs of Experience</u> and the darker, world-wise view of life. So I find Trust in God to be extremely challenging for me on both a personal and a cosmic viewpoint. In spite of the number of times that God has provided for me and taken care of my needs and allayed my fears, I still find myself inclined to visualize the very worst in store for me in the future.

Why is trust so important for faith, and can a basically cynical person even hope to gain it?

To examine the first part of that question, we need to look at the life of Jesus. It seems a bit presumptuous to hold Jesus to the standard of "Practice what you preach," but that's what I would like to do here. Does his life demonstrate the simple trusting faith of a little child that Jesus so often wishes us to have? I think his very attraction to simple souls shows some of that faith. He is attracted to Zacchaeus, who is so short that he has to climb a tree to see Jesus. There is something that reminds us of a child in the personality of Zacchaeus. Not only is he short, but he is uninhibited enough to scramble up a tree to see Jesus. He's that excited and that immune to the judgmental scorn of his contemporaries. As long as he gets to see this famous prophet, he doesn't care about the reaction, and Jesus responds to this spontaneity by calling him down and arranging to eat dinner at his house.

When the disciples argue about who is the greatest and who should be given preferential treatment when they enter the kingdom -- very adult concerns -- Jesus points out the little children who are totally uninterested in such lofty topics of power and privilege and encourages the disciples to give up their ideas of greatness and become as simple as these little children. Such simplicity is based on the trust that they are loved and protected by those they rely on. As long as they trust those who are providing for them, they have no need to fear or seek for more.

I'm told that the most popular painting of Jesus is that of the Good Shepherd, where Jesus stands with his shepherd's crook in his hand and a little sheep around his neck. People respond to this image of Jesus being there always to take care of us and protect us like the perfect shepherd. The sheep has no fear because Jesus is there to protect her. In the words of the most famous psalm: "With your rod and your staff, you protect me. I will fear no evil. Though I walk in the Valley of the Shadow of Death..."

So, in his life Jesus both embodied the trusting man of faith and pointed out the importance of trust to his disciples. That deep trust is one of the things that make the Passion such an intense experience for any Christian who enters into it with an open mind and heart. Of the various facets of the Passion, I think the most arduous one was the agony in the garden, because here was the whole of the ordeal stretching before Jesus in his mind, and for me the vision of a coming trial is always a far greater evil than the actual event. As bad as the Passion turns out to be, I can't help but think it must have played out in Jesus' mind there in Gethsemane even more vilely than it did in reality. As he sat there envisioning what he knew was coming, Jesus had to be as close as he would ever come to giving up his ideal of trusting in the Father. If he truly trusted the Father, why should he have any hesitation? The Father would, as we Christians like to blithely cant to others, not tempt him with more than he was able to bear. And yet, there is Jesus saying, if it's possible can we not do this? This is no prayer of serenity spoken by someone who has already read the end of the novel; this is agonized appeal to let the Father know that Jesus is at the end of what he can humanly suffer and endure.

If there is ever in Jesus' life a crisis of trust, it has to be at this moment, and yet ultimately even here in the extremity of his suffering, he can make the final surrender: Not my will, but yours be done. I trust as I have taught my followers to trust in the prayer I gave them, Thy will be done. I think this is the ultimate image of trust: not the frolicking lamb cavorting in the meadow under the watchful eye of the shepherd, but the totally spent and suffering Jesus accepting that God's will will always see him through even though it is not very apparent at the moment.

That gives a lot of hope to those of us who are not by nature particularly trusting. Our trust is not a condition or temperament, but an act of will. It isn't something governed by how we wake up in the morning or how we view rainbows, but rather by how in the most dire of circumstances we believe that the Lord walks with us even there. Trust then is the ultimate act of faith, saying there is a Shepherd who watches over me and will be with me all through this vale of tears under the shadow of death.

# 13 HOW ARE YOU?

So how are you doing? The worst thing, well maybe not the worst thing, but a bad thing, about books is that there is not place for feedback. When I teach a class, it is pretty easy to get feedback. I just have to look out at the students. If they're in the midst of Madden football or Snapchat or simply staring out the windows, I know that I'm not reaching them.

But here, in a book, I have no way of knowing. And you have no way of providing feedback. So here is a chapter for you to do that.

What do you think?

Are you still reading?

Anything you've seen that you like?

Anything you think is way off?

Are you going to keep reading?

What ideas of your own have you had while reading this?

Anything you want to ask me? Email me at: Michaelquillin@yahoo.com

# 14 WHY AM I SO NASTY?

I find myself much more nasty than I should be. I admire people who react in a kind and patient way in the midst of trying moments. When confronted with incompetence or indifference, they smile and tend to accept the situation for what it is instead of getting upset and demanding some sort of celestial tribunal to rule on the unfairness of it all.

And I find that the ones I am unaccountably nasty with are those closest to me. Why is it that I am least patient and loving to those who have been most kind and loving to me?

I love the way St. Paul looks at evil and us. In Romans he puts things exactly like I experience them: The good that I would like to do, I don't do, and the evil that I don't want to do, that I do. That expresses my ability to make countless resolutions on how I am going to act and then the miserable track record I compile in trying to keep those resolutions. No matter how many times I say that I am not going to let a situation or a person rile me, I find myself having the same reactions over and over. And God help the individual who would point this failing out to me!

Why do we find ourselves in this predicament and what can we do about it? Or as Paul says, Who will save me from this situation? It is Jesus. There are various step-by-step programs to get our anger and impatience under control. I know, I've tried a lot of them. My lack of progress in this area gets me ticked off, which I guess is not the point of them at all.

What is the source of the well of anger that resides inside

of us? Unfulfilled dreams, the fear that others are getting what belongs to us, the dread that our worst images of ourselves are the true ones? Whatever the source, the name for this anger that lies like a feral beast is sin. It is that sinful nature that threatens to overwhelm our better natures and implode our entire selves. This sinfulness is the violence that constitutes our daily disposition. In spite of blessings and successes, there dwells deep down that anger we fear. It remains pent up except for when it comes out.

When we're driving, for example. We're fine, sedate. Until someone crosses us or tries to cut in front of us. Then we react. Either by emotional outbursts or by actions. Road rage in the Northwest is almost a regional pastime. Stories of usually calm and even compassionate people suddenly enraged by some action are commonplace in the news.

When we're waiting. Already we're seething inward since we're being treated like cattle, forced to stand in line like a nonentity for something we really don't want anyway. And then someone pushes by us or cuts in front of us! It is not to be tolerated.

When we're at work. And we're not appreciated. The things we do are never acknowledged, and others with far less justification are preferred over us, promoted past us, fawned over even while we are ignored. It's not right.

Each of us has our measuring stick, our boiling point, our mantra calibrated to signal the breaking point. For me, it's "It's not fair!" I'm willing to put up with the absurdities of life as long as everyone else has to also, but if someone is allowed past the velvet rope without waiting his turn, I am livid. I remember a time in the Venice airport, a place not noted for its smooth-running organization, when all of us were waiting in a long serpentine line for an official to do something with our tickets or passports, or maybe to just pass judgment on the cut of our jibs. Whatever, it was a bottleneck all of us had to pass through, however long it took. A man with a couple of kids came into the group and cut into a small interstice in the line hoping to go unnoticed. No such luck. The reaction was instantaneous. People started calling out to him to get to the back of the line. The man claimed that there was an opening and that he had merely moved into it, but claiming this only fed the flames of irate emotions. The pressure of an already barely tolerable situation grew more tense and volatile because of this man's attempt to cut in front. Had not a policeman come to remove that man, there is no telling where things would have led. How does it happen that a group of basically kind human beings, people who would no doubt have helped someone who suddenly fell to the floor with a heart attack, galvanize into a mob over a very small incident? I do not mean to imply in my description that I was the detached observer. I was as outspoken and emotional as the rest -- my wife would claim more so.

This ball of evil that Paul identified so well in his own life challenges us all and turns our lives into a contest between good and evil every day of our existence. It is the evil that we would not do and yet find ourselves so ready to do. Saintliness, I think, is very much tied up with our ability to conquer this evil and re-main, not only calm, but in love with all those around us. A saint in that Venice airport would have found sympathy for that man trying to get his kids onto a plane on time instead trying to size up the logistics of drawing and quartering a person in limited space.

I'm a pessimist, or at least in my own case a realist. I don't believe that I will ever eliminate that beast massed in my soul, but I do believe I can harness it, cage it, bring it under con-trol, and the first step in that process for me is to recognize the source of evil. Why does this incident of someone cutting in line (hardly a heinous crime) bring out the very worst in me? The answer to that question certainly lies with my own fears of ad-equacy, of feeling I am someone worth being acknowledged and valued. Since I don't seem to have too strong a sense of ego in this area, I tend to react.

But knowledge is not power. That is why Paul is more perceptive than Plato, for Paul recognizes that we can know something, but still we do the other thing just as if we didn't know. I can know why I react a certain way in some situations, but that knowledge alone doesn't free me from making the wrong choice. I will still scream for blood. And that is where grace comes in, where I have to allow Jesus to lead me in a direction I do not wish to go. I will not go silently, but in my better moments I can accept the Lord's guiding me toward a calmer acceptance of the foibles of others that is based on my own recognition of my faults and shortcomings. At those flame point moments I have to seek a calmer, wiser voice than my own. Perhaps this comes through an image of Jesus suffering or a reflection of a time when I pushed someone else to the breaking point through my own insensitivity. Perhaps it's just a moment where I realize how much some people in the world are suffering and how trivial and insignificant this incident is.

Whatever the image is that I go to at this moment, the process is the same: it is a realization of my own sinfulness and a resolve to not let that weakness rule over me and a desire to put myself into God's hands to make me whole.

I don't know if this is clear to you, but I think it is necessary to confront the evil within ourselves and to find ways to combat it, and I don't think this is accomplished through brute force of will, but rather through our putting ourselves in the way of God's grace.

# 15 FEAR

Someone said once, The opposite of faith isn't faithless-ness, it's fear. It might have been Bill Barry, it might have been someone else, but among the others who said it was Jesus. He said it a lot. Do not be afraid. Peter can walk on water until he's afraid and then he sinks. The disciples can do great things once the Spirit comes to them in the upper room and removes the fear. We can move mountains with faith as long as we are not afraid to.

When I review my own life, I am struck by how much fear has ruled my actions and reactions. I'll give you an example from the present rather than dredging up ones from the past al-though many lurk in those mines. At present I volunteer once a week to visit at a hospital and to bring Communion to those who desire it. It is incredible how difficult I find this. I don't really have to do anything too demanding. I'm not called upon to do open-heart surgery or to remove a cancerous tumor; all I have to do is to visit patients who identify themselves as Cath-olics when they are admitted into the hospital. I simply go in, talk to them, and if they desire it, I give them Communion.

Simple, and yet I have a tough time with it. Why? Well, there is fear somewhere in this process, but I can't really iden-tify it. Certainly I am not like the first apostles who went forth and preached and knew that they were at risk of rejection and even death. And yet they did it gladly. I knock and enter each room hesitantly, reluctantly, making up excuses to leave even before I have met the patient.

How do I deal with this fear?

First, I have to admit it. It is no good pretending that I

don't experience it. It is a part of who I am. But, next, after I have admitted feeling that fear, I cannot let it own me. That fear cannot dictate my actions. Because I have this nameless fear, I can't avoid going into a room and greeting a patient. I can see the fear and understand how it is working on me without giving into the repercussions and paralysis that fear can cause in me. Once I know I am fearful I am better able to limit its effect on me. Partly that comes from self-knowledge and partly that comes from my ability to ask God for fortitude. I love that old-fashioned word which is perfect for this context. I say, "Jesus, you know what a coward I can be. Help me now by giving me your Spirit to continue on, to live in the moment and not try to rush through it or avoid it or anesthetize myself from living this moment fully. It is you who lives in me."

Somehow, that prayer centers me and calms me. It's a bit of Zen, but it's also more the realization that I live outside myself in Jesus and his grace guides me. It is a bit galling to admit that I need help to overcome my fears. I like to picture myself as a strong, independent person who can face all of my difficulties on my own; to have to call upon Jesus to strengthen me during this time of distress goes against my rugged individualism image, and yet it is the reality of the situation. I do need the power of grace to help me to escape the prison of my own fears. In calling upon another I become more fully myself beyond what I could have accomplished without doing so.

Peter, filled with the desire to be with Jesus, walks upon the water toward him. It is only when he becomes conscious of what he is doing and starts to fear that he sinks. Jesus must have been laughing at that moment when he reaches down to Peter and asks why he suddenly started to fear. With us the Lord must frequently wonder why we are fearful when so many times in the past he has been there for us when we needed him.

Of the many obstacles to faith in the Gospels, fear must rank as the strongest, most difficult to overcome. Again and again, followers of Jesus leave him when they fear what his message might cost them. The rich young man who wants to know what he can do to live an even better life is caught up in this. Jesus looks at him and loves him. He sees the wonderful possibilities in this idealistic young man and so he tells him frankly what is required: Go, sell what you have and come follow me. It is starkly put; there is no ambiguity, no ambivalence about how to interpret this message. Get rid of what you have and come with me. What might have happened if that young man had done exactly that. But he doesn't; the fear holds him back. What will I be like if I don't have all of these things? How will I get along? If it doesn't work out, how will I ever again acquire all of these wonderful possessions? I can't take that chance, I'm afraid.

And so he walks away. What happens to him, we don't know. Maybe he led a perfectly acceptable life, but he never walked with Jesus, he never knew the hardships and sorrows, but he also never knew the triumphs that could have been his if he left behind his fear and believed.

So many times in my life I am confronted with the same choice between fear of losing my comfortable situation and the possibility of so much more in following Jesus.

# 16 THE STRANGER

Who constitutes a stranger in your life? How has he or she acquired that status? That Manicheaean split again. Some are us and the others aren't.

I remember a teacher telling me a story once of an incident that happened in the school cafeteria. Two groups, one African American, one White, got into a confrontation that threatened to turn violent. After the teacher had calmed the situation a bit, he took a few of the main students away from the scene and asked them what had happened. One of the kids said, "See we were sitting there, and they. . ." And the teacher interrupted him. He said, "No, what happened?" And another kid said, "We weren't doing anything and then they . . ." And again the teacher stopped him. The students were puzzled, but another tried, "See, they . . ." And again the teacher cut in. It took the students a long time to realize what he was doing. The teacher wasn't going to allow anyone to relate the event in terms of us and them, and that was the crux of the whole issue. Once they weren't allowed to look at the problem as a matter our side and theirs, us and them, their whole vocabulary for recounting the event crumbled. They were no longer able to express the dynamics of the case since the false dichotomy raised in the minds of the participants fell apart. It wasn't us and them, it was only us, who had a problem with ourselves, and that was infinitely easier to deal with.

Once we can shed that dichotomy of us and them, the solutions to problems become much clearer and more attainable. We see more accurately the true situation where we are connected to the other, that their happiness in some way determines our happiness, and when they are suffering we all suffer. It's a hard lesson to attain, but a good one.

It is a lesson learned in increments. Just as we are able to expand our circle of We, we come up against another group of They that we find it hard to include. Just as we learn to reach out to the homeless in our city we are confronted with the homeless in the whole country or the world. Just as we give to those in need, we find ourselves reacting against those who aren't polite or thankful, who don't appreciate what we're doing for them or how good and generous we are. There is always some group beyond our circle that the Lord calls on us to welcome into the safety of our love.

One of the ancient monastic orders had a saying, "When a stranger comes to the door, Christ comes to the door." The way we treat this stranger is the way we treat Christ. An almost word for word application of Jesus' admonition to us in the Sermon on the Mount, where he says that clothing the naked or feeding the hungry is caring for Jesus and neglecting these needy is neglecting Jesus.

The importance of the stranger in our own spirituality is seen in Pope Francis' idea that we work our salvation out as a community. Now the stranger becomes someone much more central to our lives. He isn't someone we can literally take or leave; he becomes central to our own salvation. If we leave him behind, we leave Jesus behind, we leave our own salvation behind. Now we are spurred into action in a very critical way. It's a matter of the utmost importance that we help this stranger, if only because by doing so we are helping ourselves, or to put it more theologically, we are helping Jesus (A stranger comes, Jesus comes. Whatever you do for the least of my sisters, you do for me.) Seeing the stranger, not as other, but as Jesus revises our whole way of thinking just as the loss of the we/they paradigm changed the way the students looked at their confrontation.

Who are the strangers in my life? Whom do I fear or suspect or choose to avoid? Or, just as bad, whom do I fail to see as people other than being there to serve my needs and make me

# happy?

# 17 PAY ATTENTION!

As a teacher I have been aware of the problem of paying attention my whole life. The constant struggle of a teacher is to find ways to hold the attention of her audience. If one is truly honest in observing behavior, she has to admit that it is impossible to hold the attention of say 25 very different personalities at the same time for very long. A dramatic moment might rivet attention, but that quickly melts away into a number of different paths away from the shrine. That momentary fascination quickly turns to other concerns and activities. In moments of teaching brilliance -- and I assure you I was brilliant at least in my mind -- I will get interrupted by the hand wanting to know if he can go to the bathroom. In the midst of an insight that will change the lives of my students forever, I detect someone checking email, looking up what class is next or just plain shaking his watch to make sure it's still working.

Here's a true to life illustration that any teacher can instantly recognize. Five, ten years after you have had a student in one of your classes, you run into him somewhere, and he says, "Oh, I remember your class! Remember the time you threw Robbie's backpack out the window?" Of all the things that happened during that semester, the only thing that remained in his mind was some random incident.

And if someone were naive enough to consider this a fault only of the young, simply observe the actions of your contemporaries in similar circumstances. Nothing is more embarrassing than to witness the behavior of a roomful of teachers at a faculty meeting. Ones who demand absolute attention and no external sign of wandering minds demonstrate an almost total inability to follow even the simplest presentation for a short period of time.

As a further, quite painful illustration of this point, just reflect for a moment on how your attention has been flitting in and out as you try to read this section of the book or the book in general. If you're honest, a bit spotty, right? Please, don't write to tell me how badly your attention has waned, I can't deal with that much truth.

But paying attention here is not about participating in a class or lecture; it is about paying attention to our lives. I always liked the bumper sticker that warned, "If you're not outraged, you haven't been paying attention." I find I can live large sections of my life without paying attention. I can seem to go along without even paying any regard to what I'm doing or how I'm doing it and certainly not at all why I'm doing it. I think that was the great insight of Socrates: there is nothing that happens in your life that shouldn't come under scrutiny. Everything you think and hold to be true should be examined; every action or project you undertake should be able to be defended against any objections. Reading Plato's *Dialogues*, I always thought that I would have to kill Socrates if I lived with him day in and day out. Life just can't be that scrutinized, that dissected by this unflinching gaze. And yet, who can deny the brilliance of Socrates's insight? If we don't pay attention to our lives, we are subject to any outside winds that might blow down our streets. If we don't examine why we hold a particular viewpoint, how can we ever get into a position where we can refine or even change that opinion?

Jesus also calls us to pay attention to our world, to what we believe about that world, what we choose to look at and what we are willing to participate in. For a Christian, paying attention means looking beyond our own little sphere or life and seeing what is going on in the greater world around us. It means realizing that we are part of that world whether we want to be or not and that we are called again and again through many mouths to look at all of that. I find that I can easily escape from paying attention to things I don't want to face. Much like the person who averts his eyes during a gruesome scene on TV, I can turn quickly away from something too awful to face. I remember as part of a training program in Pastoral Care, I was invited to witness a birth. I didn't make it. The director took one look at me, whiter than the mask I was wearing and suggested that maybe I should step outside for a breather. I'm a light-weight when it comes to witnessing human suffering. Any number of times when I am visiting someone in the hospital, I will wish that they would stop relating to me in great detail what happened in the motorcycle accident or the fall from the ladder.

But this lack of paying attention covers a wider range and a longer period of time. We do not want to pay attention to the suffering in the world. The current disaster faced by thousands of people stranded somewhere between the land they left and safety in a some country that would accept them is a calamity that seems old to me now. A year or more back it was front page news, but now we have tired of it, and it no longer makes headlines. And yet, we know that the plight of these homeless refugees continues. I know that people continue to be displaced (an awful term suggesting they are pieces of furniture inexpertly deployed), and that they need our help. And yet we stop paying attention. We move on to other, hopefully more pleasant, thoughts. Being of faith demands that we pay attention. These things are occurring, with or without our witnessing. Jesus says, Look!

Probably the most misused quote in the Bible is Jesus' comment, "The poor you always have with you." This isn't a dismissal that it's not worth it to try to eradicate poverty since we'll always have the problem, no matter how hard we try, it's a fact. They are always there. Pay attention. You might think they're gone, but they're not, they are always here. Look! Don't just stand there, do something.

And that's the next step in paying attention: Do something. We can't really be Christians if we don't pay attention, if we don't see what is going on and do something about it. That action might take different forms and it won't always be directly connected to that particular problem, but it will in some way be a response to the issue. It will say that as followers of Jesus we are paying attention to what he is saying and more importantly what he is doing and imitating him by going forth and doing likewise.

# 18 HOPE

"If God is for us, who can be against us?"
Romans 8

This question of Paul's from his letter to the Romans has always been a calming, comforting thought that has brought me hope in some of my darkest times. I love the logic of it: either you believe or you don't. If you do, then what do you believe? Who do you think the God you believe in is? If indeed your God is one who loves you, what more do you need? If this God is for you, what else is there?

Hope is the call to rely on that bedrock insight, to stay confident even when all logic tells you to bail. When every sign points to staying as you are, warm and comfortable in the world you have created, hope calls you to grow, to take a chance and answer God's call to become someone more.

The Bible is littered with people who faced the same dilemma and answered God's call: Leave home and follow me. For Abraham, God said, Leave home, lead a people to the promised land. Father a great nation, even though you and Sarai are old. Sacrifice a son, even though he is your only chance at this great nation.

Peter is told, Leave your nets, come follow me, learn to fish for something greater. John and Andrew: Come and see.

Each time the temptation was to stay put, to say, I know best what I need to be happy. Change is uncomfortable, risky, chancy. But these people did not sink back into that comfort and security of their prior life. Hope is the belief that God has greater plans for me than I could ever imagine. Hope poses to the individual a very real existential decision: Is life a series of random events or does God truly rule time and lead us ultimately toward salvation? Hope answers that question one way: Hope that we are moving toward something better.

Hope is such an important virtue in the modern world. Because we know so much of every bad thing that occurs in our world, it is so easy to lose the hope that we are indeed moving toward a more perfect world of salvation. An evening of watching the network newscasts can leave Mary Poppins reaching for the Scotch bottle. As we look at events on the local and national and international stages, we can't help feeling worried for our future and the future of the everyone. The optimism that Jesus expresses between his resurrection and his ascension seems like a message from a far distant kingdom.

When I think of hope, I frequently focus on Peter, a man not usually associated with that virtue. But think of Peter's situation in life and his response to it. Let's just take it from his actions when Jesus is arrested and then eventually crucified. During that period Peter is hardly a paragon of loyalty. He follows at a distance. In spite of boasts to the contrary, he is not at Jesus' side and when confronted, he denies even being associated with Jesus. By the time of the Crucifixion Peter must have been in deep despondent darkness. What could rally him from this depression?

The Resurrection, which Peter was not among the first to embrace, must have come as a tremendous act of redemption for Peter, and yet some of Jesus' words to him are less than thrilling: "Truly, truly, I say to you, when you were young, you used to dress yourself and walk wherever you wanted, but when you are old, you will stretch out your hands, and another will dress you and carry you where you do not want to go."

Hardly the message of optimism on which to build a career! A stark, disconcerting view into a future that could not have made Peter emboldened to rush into his destiny. To be handed over and mistreated by your enemies without any say in the process is what most of us fear for our future. A modern equivalent is that fear of sitting untended, unwatched, unloved in the hallways of some low-rent nursing home that is little more than a holding tank for the soon-to-be-departed. Someone to uncaringly dress us in the morning (if that) and abandon us to the hinterlands of an anonymous facility to be fetched back to a stark room in the evening, banished to the life of sitcoms and quiz shows. This is not the stuff of dreams and hopes.

And yet hope is what Peter has, the hope that drives him to heal beggars and preach the message of Christ crucified and resurrected, to foster the growth of the fledgling Church and to spend all of his energy ensuring that the world does not forget who Jesus was or what he had to teach us. His life, in spite of such obstacles, is one of great hope for us today. When we look at the obstacles that he overcame to believe and hope still, we realize that our modern situation is not much different. While there are few indicators that the world is getting holier or happier, we continue to hope that God's Kingdom on earth is arriving.

Besides the plight of Peter, the other image I have of hope is that of Mary and John at the foot of the Cross. What thoughts must have been going through the minds of the two of them as they stood there looking upon Jesus. This was more than the death of the hope that all of the disciples and followers had; this was the death of one's own son, one's best friend. All of the great moments and aspirations seemed wiped away in one cruel, relentless calamity. What must have been the thoughts of Mary as she looked on? And of John?

And of the disciples on their way to Emmaus? How could they maintain any hope after their journey up to Jerusalem only to have their dreams shattered by the Crucifixion? How could hope be possible in the face of such a harsh reality?

And yet for each of them, there was a greater reality than they could imagine waiting for them. This reality could not have unfolded without the prior disappointment that asked them to hope in the future. Their hope is rewarded by a new, vibrant reality. Hope then is the belief that God has greater plans for me than I could ever imagine.

ASSIGNMENT: MEDITATE on this passage:

"For in this hope we were saved. Now hope that is seen is not hope. For who hopes for what he sees? But if we hope for what we do not see, we wait for it with patience.

And we know that for those who love God all things work together for good, for those who are called according to his purpose.

What then shall we say to these things? If God is for us, who can be against us?

Who shall separate us from the love of Christ? Shall tribulation, or distress, or persecution, or famine, or nakedness, or danger, or sword?

For I am sure that neither death nor life, nor angels nor rulers, nor things present nor things to come, nor powers, nor height nor depth, nor anything else in all creation, will be able to separate us from the love of God in Christ Jesus our Lord." (Romans 8:24-39 ESV)

Jesus is standing before you. What is he asking of you in terms of hope? What is your response?

# 19 SIMPLICITY

Simplicity seems such an old fashioned virtue, something left over from an earlier time when children were to be seen and not heard, where being patient and unassuming and in the background was a thing to be prized. The virtue does not easily translate into the modern world where strident claims for attention and action are called for. The word itself conjures up images of being feeble minded or unadventurous. One is simple because he hasn't seen enough of the world to appreciate the multiplicity and wonder of it.

Langston Hughes, a much underappreciated writer, has a set of stories about a character named Simple. Today they are probably not very often read and are perhaps open to much misperceptions, but at its essence the character is someone whose heart is pure. We have, I think, all known similar people, those with simple, unfeigned emotions, with hearts that quickly and totally reach out to embrace others, who suspect no evil in others and act out of the goodness of their own hearts. This is not a description of the type of person parents want their children to grow up to be. The world is too wily, too nefarious, too threatening to send children out into the wolves' den with the innocence of lambs.

Yet, innocence is not quite so vulnerable as we cynics believe. The real attraction of the virtue is its indissolubility, its rugged integrity that cannot be broken down further. To be truly simple requires a great deal of strength and independence. It is hard, shiny, irreducible as a diamond. It can remain impervious and indomitable in a sea of turbulence where more stalwart ships are scuttled. The simple saint of pure heart and vibrant love can undergo and survive the sternest tests of life. We frequently encounter stories about simple people who pursue wholly unreachable goals only to eventually succeed against all odds. He hear those stories and we credit them, but we really don't see them as applicable to our lives. We are too worldly wise and too sophisticated to go down that road.

But still the virtue of simplicity has a draw for our lives. It calls us to articulate in a few words what we truly believe in and what we think life is all about. Maybe it is not as simple as the banners we hung in our dorm rooms at college or wrote in our notebooks, but simplicity demands a huge response from us: What do you believe? It is easy enough to critique other people and movements, to say that such and such an approach is futile, but what do you offer in opposition as an alternative? What do you stand for? What value is paramount in your life as you live it? I leave that "value" as singular because simplicity calls for it to be so.

If you had to name one value that stands out in your life, what would it be? Honesty? Loyalty? What? Or do you refuse to play this game, to allow your life to be reduced to one value? The simple person would not back away from that question and she would not fear the ridicule and second-guessing of those on the sidelines. She would say what she stood for and be at peace with it.

Stop reading. Well, of course, you can't stop reading and still know what to do next. It's like when I would have my students create meditations. They would start out with, "Close your eyes." And then continue with a number of directions that no one could follow if they really closed their eyes. So, stop reading, but keep going. Review the major phases of your life. Throughout, what has been the value you have tried to adhere to throughout? What is the salient virtue that you could say you have shown? Sure, you may not always have succeeded in living up to it, but you have always tried to be what? When have you been most forceful in living up to that virtue? When have you been furthest from embodying it? What are the factors that foster or defeat the simple goodness of your life?

As you reflect on the simple truth of your life, are you happy with it? Are you still a person seeking to live a life that exemplifies this virtue? What can you do now to make your proclamation of this virtue stronger, more pronounced?

# 20 ORDINARY TIME

My favorite time of the Church calendar is Ordinary Time. And yes, I do like vanilla ice cream. There is something quiet and comforting about that period in the Church year. The pews aren't full of people crammed in for Easter or Christmas, in fact they aren't full at all. There's only the usual assortment of folks who gravitate to their usual part of the Church and following their accustomed rituals of preparing for and following the liturgy. There's no great event or earth-shaking homily, just the usual murmur and hum of an ordinary Sunday beginning the ordinary week.

But it is in the ordinary that we most often follow the Lord, listening to his Word, comparing it to our own following of it, finding it wanting, resolving to do better, knowing that we probably won't, that our failings of the past weeks will still be there in the coming weeks even though we really will try. Ordinary time is, I think, like much of the Gospels, where the disciples just followed Jesus from town to town trying to make sense of his parables and understand what the kingdom means for them. These were just regular stretches filled with quotidian tasks of finding bread and wine and fishes, locating places to stay, and trying hard to learn the life of a disciple.

Faith for most of us is a matter of doing the everyday things well. Mother Teresa said something like that when she pointed out that love consisted in doing the little things well. Most of our lives is consumed with the small things, the seemingly insignificant parts that we look back on and realize comprised our lives and gave them meaning. The grand gestures, while magnificent in scope, are few and far between in most of our lives. The poignant declarations of love, while thrilling, mean less in the long run than the small sacrifices and errands that fill our waking hours and make a relationship continue to endure and thrive.

I might be transported in a moment of rapture in prayer, but much more important is that daily resolution to pray even though I am distracted by bigger issues like whether to take advantage of Amazon's Deal of the Day. In one of J.D. Salinger's books, I think it's *Franny and Zooey,* he says that it's easier to die for a cause than to live for it day after day. It's true for me. I can visualize taking a dramatic stand that announces to the world my courageous faith in the Lord, but it's harder to get up Sunday after Sunday to make it to Mass. It's harder to be kind to that annoying colleague who seems to live his life in a way engineered to irk me the most.

Ordinary Time! That's when we make the choices that are the seeds germinating unnoticed beneath the soil that lead to the Easter lilies and Christmas poinsettias. Ordinary Time, when we, as the Psalmist reminds us, "Seek the Lord while he may be found." The injunction says it all. We can waste our lives waiting for the big moments, but now in the small, brown moments the Lord can be found, and you need to seek him now. He won't always be there for the taking, you can't decide to wait and expect the Lord to still be there. You can't say, one of these days I'm going to help with that bread line or volunteer at my daughter's soccer program or tutor a student, but not now. You can be bored during Ordinary Time and wait for the big moment, but the Lord is to be found NOW in the ordinary moment. Seek him while he may be found.

# 21 FAITH

When a person is checked into a hospital, many times they will be asked, along with other information, what religion they are. A fair number of patients will check Catholic, even here in Washington, which is one of the two most unchurched states in the union, i.e. the most people who consider themselves as belonging to no religious denomination. When visiting these patients, I find a wide range of Catholics though. There are those, at one end of the spectrum, who are glad to see you and willingly ask to receive Communion. At the other end, there are those who are surprised that they marked Catholic and are polite, but no thank you, they haven't really been Catholic for years and don't feel the need to renew the affiliation at this time.

What does it mean to say you are a Catholic today?

When I look at that question I just wrote, I am not happy with it. It is somehow a lifeless question when the issue is anything but lifeless, it is at the heart of life, just as starkly as when Moses lays it out for the people in Deuteronomy: "I call heaven and earth to witness against you today, that I have set before you life and death, blessing and curse." Therefore choose life, that you and your offspring may live." (Deut. 30:19).

I would phrase the above question differently so that it carries more of an immediate significance. I would put it this way:

The question of whether God exists is the most critical in any person's life. Whether we believe, whether we know, or whether we remain in doubt, each one of us seeks to bring to light the meaning of our own existence. Each one of us strives to discover whether there is something outside the person, something that made the world come into existence and to assume the form it has assumed.

It is where Ignatius starts the <u>Exercises </u>because it is the all-important question. Do you accept that God exists, not just in an abstract, remote way, but intensely in your life? It is the starting point of the old Baltimore Catechism, which asked why did God make me? From that answer so many paths fan out for us to explore, but they are not all the same and cannot be followed injudiciously. We fan out from this focal point in the direction our answer sends us. If you answer that there is no God, I do not know where that will lead you except to say that it will lead you in a different direction from the one this book will go.

If you answer that you believe that there is a God in your life, there is still a wide variety of ways you may proceed, but at least we have a starting point. Let us take a look for a moment at some of the ramifications of our acceptance.

If we accept that we come from God, we accept our position as creatures of God. We are daughters and sons of God who are born with relationships and responsibilities just as being born into any family does. Accepting that I am a child of God means I accept that I come from God and I go back to God in my journey in life. All of the people I meet along the way are my brothers and sisters and I hold a responsibility for them and their condition and their happiness. I cannot be oblivious to their existence and their needs.

This realization creates an attitude of humility. I am not the center of the universe. I am not the only point of brilliance in God's universe, but merely part of that brilliance, one little pixel in the vast glorious screen of beauty and color. Instead of inculcating a peacock pride, my realization fosters a sense of kinship and empathy with all other creatures.

Along with humility, this realization of being from God creates a spirit of thankfulness for my own being. Recognizing God as the source of all, I respond with a grateful resolve to live life to the fullest in an embrace of his creation. This is not the hang gliding live life of the beer ads, but rather the resolve to go forth into the world and do those things that God intended for us from the start: to love and be loved, to protect and nourish and bring peace throughout God's creation.

We are filled with the certainty that God loves us. We are not here just to fill a place, just to be a number. We are, as in Hosea's vision, known by God from the womb. He has chosen us for a purpose. In faith we know this and this understanding suffuses every aspect of our existence.

Your life is not so much about you as it is about what God is doing through you.

# 22 FAITH AND GOOD WORKS

*Faith or good works. Are we just another service organization?*

A long-running debate within the Church between traditionalists and more progressive elements is the one about how much the Church should be involved in social activism as opposed to conventional religious matters. The fear at one end of the spectrum is that the Church could become merely another secular service organization or even worse become identified with one political party to the exclusion of its mission to be universal in its message to all.

A look at modern retreats and renewals certainly provides reason to be wary. The slogans and goals of many of these activities emphasize the values of teamwork, community, awareness, and volunteerism. All of these are worthy goals, but are they specifically tied to the Church and its mission? Could we not just as easily accomplish these ends under the aegis of some more political or social institution? What makes such activities uniquely Christian if much the same work is carried on by a panoply of other organizations and services?

Activities aren't different; motivations are. I volunteer at a place that provides immediate, temporary aid to the homeless in Seattle. The actions this place, St. Francis House, does are not really different from those of many other similar sites in Seattle and around the country. How then is this a Christian activity? Aside from a prayer at the opening of the house in the morning and scattered iconography throughout the place, there is not a uniquely Christian pedigree to the endeavor and certainly many of the people who move through St. Francis House during the day are unaware of its Christian roots. But I would argue that the difference lies in the motivation for these actions rather than the actions themselves. The same acts of feeding the hungry and clothing the naked are carried out because the actors are responding to the message of Jesus, who sent us out to do these acts in the name of the Father and in imitation of Him.

Such a distinction may not be apparent to an outsider, but it is clearly the difference for the person performing the actions. She is striving toward a more equitable world as a response to the Gospel message: Go forth and recreate the world. It is a life consisting of love-based action, a following in Jesus' footsteps. Like the washing of the feet commemorated on Holy Thursday, we are called to do these things because Jesus did them.

The difference is more than one of perception. Traditionally, Christianity has always seen work as something that is entwined with prayer. In the Benedictine motto, the ideal of the Christian vocation is to work and to prayer. The two nourish each other, our prayer giving meaning to our work and our work validating our prayer. As John and Timothy stress in their letters, Christians who claim to love God but fail to minister to their needs are living a lie.

In the same way that work validates our prayer life relationship with God, so our prayer gives purpose and form to our works. Because we are motivated by our love of God we are not dependent on the love of those we serve. We are undeterred when our efforts are not acknowledged. If those we serve do not thank us, we remember Christ's words that it is the particular insight of Christianity to help those who are in need, but not particularly admirable. Our thanks comes from another source, and so our need for immediate gratification is lessened and we are not tempted to give up our efforts when they do not result in positive receptions measured by earthly terms.

So when one views the posters and agenda for a youth

retreat or a service weekend, it is easy to cynically dismiss the activity of mere social service with a light patina of Christianity spread across the top, but the true answer to such a situation is much harder to ascertain. Is there within the activity an attempt to tie such service and other-directed charity to the gospel of Jesus? Sometimes that association is quite tenuous, even in the pre-evangelization stage of things, but nevertheless there is the hope of bringing our consciousnesses to a deeper realization of the message of the Lord and of our proper response to that message.

This kind of work rooted in prayer is the foundation of Ignatius's injunction to pray without ceasing. As mentioned earlier, our work becomes an expression of our closeness to God and so a form of praying too. It lifts the apparently mundane activity to a new level of being, one more closely united to God.

# 23 SURPRISE

Surprise isn't something you immediately associate with spirituality. With all of the repetition mentioned earlier, it's difficult to think of arriving to Mass and being surprised by much. Yet, I think that surprise must have been much at the heart of the early Church. Certainly the apostles' experience of traveling with Jesus had to be studded with surprises. To get in a boat to cross a lake leaving Jesus behind only to find him on the other side later on had to be a head scratcher for them. Not to mention seeing him walk on the water. In almost any of the towns they entered Jesus had to surprise them with his behavior, whether it was spending time with and healing a beggar or deciding to have dinner with known disreputable ones. The element of surprise had to suffuse the entire experience of following Jesus for the disciples.

The greatest surprise, though, would be the Resurrection. At the moment of abject despair, to be jolted into a new awareness of Jesus risen from the dead and back among them must have topped any other surprise that the followers of Jesus could have experienced. What must have been their feelings as they stood around dumbfounded in the presence of Jesus? And he subverts the entire majesty of the moment by the plebeian question, "Got something to eat?" Jesus' coming back among the disciples who had lost all hope of a Messiah certainly surprised all of them beyond any expectation.

While the liturgical year, with its circular repetitions, doesn't seem to provide much in the way of surprises, there is much more possibility than we realize. In Orthodoxy, G.K. Chesterton, the great proponent of the paradox, makes the case that something that happens over and over doesn't necessarily remove the miraculous nature of it. Just because it repeats itself, that doesn't mean that the event isn't as spectacular as the very first time. He uses as one of his examples the sunrise. The fact that each and every day the sun has come up, he argues, is no guarantee that it will rise this morning, and so we await it and are thrilled anew by its coming, no less dramatically than any of the other mornings. It is all in our attitude, in our capacity to be thrilled again.

For those open to the possibilities, belief in Jesus and his saving power can also open a person up to immense vistas far beyond what the merely rational mind could comprehend. In the area of what we can accomplish or overcome, our faith can make possible great things. The mustard seed of faith, as Jesus predicted, can indeed move mountains when it needs to. The stories of healing that constitute much of the Gospels don't end there. Even today more miracles of faith continue to be accomplished by those who believe and hope. The surprise of faith in God still awaits us in many forms.

But I don't want to limit the dimension of surprise to the healing of the sick and the blind. It affects more than the Sunday morning program replete with casting aside the crutches. The true surprise of the Gospels is not the healing of the lepers and the lame, it is the transformation of the many people who heard Jesus speak and believed and followed him. The true surprise for us lies in the less spectacular but as essential change in our hearts as we hear the message of Jesus and strive to follow him. These surprises transform the world not through stunning feats of superhuman ability but through the small, hidden acts of kindness that turn us outward from our selfish worries into the greater world of need. These humble, everyday actions are the true surprises because of their accumulated effect in the world.

These acts surprise the receiver who did not expect them, but they surprise us too because we did not think ourselves capable of them. Yet in Christ, we can Surprise! Do all things.

# 24 GRACE

Grace is a tough enough topic that great minds have struggled over the centuries to define it and to explain its importance. For all of its importance as a bone of contention, grace remains an evanescent concept. When we talk about faith, hope or charity, we may have different definitions of these terms, but most people would think that they know what they mean when they use them. Not so grace.

What does the term mean? What is grace? Is it a quality or characteristic or an outside agency? Is it something we have inside ourselves that grows and develops as we do? Or is it something given to us from outside in gradually increasing quantities?

Jesus says, "Grace I give unto you." The saints pray for various graces. St. Ignatius sets up his <u>Spiritual Exercises</u> to pray for a particular grace. So the term is bruited about a great deal, and yet for all of the amazing definitions of grace I have heard over the years, grace is not a concept I have a clear understanding of. It is truly one of those things that I walk away after hearing it explained and think, "Wow, I finally get it." Only to wake up the next day as clueless as ever.

So, here is my explanation of grace, one you can also say Wow! And then later remain puzzled by the term.

Grace is the enabler. I know that that is a terrible word since it has so many negative connotations, but it is the best I can come up with at the moment. Grace is what helps us do what we couldn't do on our own. Paul in <u>Romans</u> explains it best. He starts by perfectly describing the situation of many of us. We want to do the right thing and to avoid the wrong thing, but just the opposite happens. That which we don't want to do we do, and that which we want to do we don't. It sounds like doublespeak except that when we read it, we know exactly what Paul is talking about. It's just so easy to go contrary to the direction we want to move in. Whatever aspect of life we want to improve in we find ourselves meeting obstacles and sliding back into the swamp of recidivism.

And Paul expresses it perfectly: Who will rescue me from this dilemma, this living hell? Who, in effect, can save me from myself? In our very efforts to extricate ourselves, we build the walls of our prison and make us more and more deeply isolated from any help. The very idea that we can by ourselves deliver us from evil condemns us to this fate. There is, it seems, no escape from our self-made prison -- except for grace.

Ah, Grace. Without grace we are trapped in an eternity of failure. We can't will ourselves into sanctity. We know what we should do, but we can't seem to accomplish it on our own. That is where grace comes in. We can with grace accomplish that which we could never attain unaided. Again, it seems like we are making up an agency outside of ourselves to thank for what ultimately comes only from our inner reserves. And for someone who insists on only what we can demonstrate, I have no answer except that process of faith that operates beyond what we can analyze and prove. Grace allowed Paul to step outside his paralysis of sin to walk in the light of Christ.

And so it does with us. Grace enables us to follow Christ in spite of our many failings and blind spots and prejudices. We are better than we could be because of the gift of grace from Our Lord.

And grace is a gift. As people like Martin Luther stressed so eloquently, it is truly a gift, perhaps the purest gift imaginable since we can in no way work hard enough to earn it. It comes to us without any proof of merit on our part, and our only response is to receive it and cherish it and to enjoy it. It is not in our nature to be in debt to someone else. We would prefer that grace were a prize winnable by so many points of good deeds or holy thoughts, but alas it is not. The message of Paul and Luther and others is that grace comes to us because of God's love, not our worthiness. We can't enter a spiritual gym and bulk up on reps that will ultimately qualify us as grace-worthy.

That's alarming in one sense and totally freeing if we look at it in another way. We have nothing to do but be thankful. That thankfulness invites us to bask in the freely given grace from God, but there is a caveat here: This is not Cheap Grace, as Bonhoeffer calls it, where we are simply dispensed our portion without any strings attached. We cannot hear the tales of others' misfortunes and smugly reflect that we are so much better because we live holier lives. We are not free to say God is love; I am saved and that is it. Truly accepting God's grace calls upon us to respond. We cannot fully explore God's love to us without being compelled to respond, just as we cannot love and be loved by another person and remain unchanged. Being blessed by grace impels us to share that gift with others. Once we see how God has loved us, we ask what response we can make for this wonderful gift. And the answer is to love Him back, just as it is with any love. But, as John in his letters points out, we express this love for God by loving his creatures. We love God and we show this by doing loving acts whenever and wherever we can. Those who don't, those who say they love God, but don't show this love in deeds are liars.

Grace is both the easiest and the hardest of Christian concepts. It is hard, because we can't seem to get it no matter how hard we work at it. It is like pursuing the horizon to those who feel all things worth having are worth working hard for. The harder we try, the further away it seems. And yet it is infinitely easy for those who simply accept. For the one who stops trying to wrestle it to the ground and just steps back and puts out her arms, it is all given to her in a wonderful, abundant bouquet of freely granted blessings.

Grace is just stopping long enough to let God love us. It is, Anthony de Mello says somewhere about prayer, simply stepping back and looking at God and letting God look back at us and smile. I like that idea for prayer, but I like it even better for grace: Grace is God's smile for us. It is God looking at us and saying, I like you, you make me smile. And our only response can be, Thanks. That's all I need, your smile.

# 25 JOB AND EVIL

To me the most fascinating book of the O.T. is the Book of Job. It is so perfect in the questions it asks and honest in the attempts to answer those questions:

Why do evil people seem to prosper while just ones seem to suffer?

Why suffering?

When I talk to people -- young or older -- about why they no longer believe, I get one response more than any other: I used to believe until (Fill in the blank with whatever evil thing happened to them or their loved ones.) I can't believe in a God who would let that happen to such a good person, they would say. Give me a good reason why and I will believe, they challenge.

When I was young and knew everything, I spent a summer working in the chaplain's office of a large hospital in the heart of Chicago. Because of its location, it received some of the most severe and heart-rending cases that a big city can dredge up in a long, trying summer.

One of the tasks for this program was to stay overnight to answer any emergency calls. On one of those nights I was called down to the Emergency Room. There I met an hysterical mother who couldn't have been any older than I at 26. Her daughter of about 5 had run out in the street and been immediately killed by a car. When I saw the girl, it seemed almost impossible to imagine. She was beautiful and almost unaltered in appearance by the accident. She lay there almost as if asleep, and yet she was fatally and irreversibly dead, never more to be a part of this mother's world.

My job was to comfort the mother, to help her to feel at

peace with what was something that had no comfort, no peace about it. As she cried and sobbed and asked why, why, why, I was supposed to come up with some formula that would solve all of this pain for her. I was helpless. As the mother raved wanting to see her child, all of the professionals around me looked on as if to say, "Do your job. Quiet her down. We did ours; now it's your turn. Make her stop screaming."

I was clueless. No matter what I said, it made not difference. The mother continued to cry. Finally, I fell back on the cliche, "She's in a better place now."

That did the trick; she stopped crying. But not the way I wanted it. She looked at me with incomprehension. She couldn't believe what she had heard. She looked at me like I was newly arrived on this planet and said, "A better place? She was in a better place with me. What do you mean a better place." And with that she started wailing again.

I resolved then and there to never try to assuage someone's pain through an anodyne saying that I myself really didn't believe. I said I would never settle for a greeting card approach to death or pain or evil that coated it over with a glib one-liner.

Which brings me to the Book of Job.

The story itself is an odd-ball account since it doesn't seem to arise out of the Jewish tradition, but is rather plucked from another culture nearby. How it came to be included in the books of the Bible is anyone's guess, and there are those who, seeing the view of God presented, would just as soon if it hadn't been. From the start, the book sets a strange tone. God is anthropomorphized as few other places in the Bible. He is sitting around with his cronies more or less passing the time telling stories when, of all characters, Satan shows up. Rather than being the major confrontation one would expect, the two converse quite amicably. To God's boast about his servant Job, Satan replies that sure, Job is faithful, why wouldn't he be? Look at all God has given to him. But take that away and then see what would happen, your buddy wouldn't be so quick to sing God's praises then.

And so God allows Satan to take away everything from Job: his sheep, his cows, his buildings and lands and crops, even his children, but still Job stays faithful: Naked I came from my mother's womb; naked shall I return. God is vindicated, but Satan is undeterred. Sure Job is faithful, but touch his body and then see how he will howl. And so God allows Satan to cover Job with sores, to take away everything and leave Job covered with sores and sitting on a dunghill. Still Job refuses to blame God.

Underneath the folksy imagery of the story lies the horrible truth: for no reason other than the whim of a bet with Satan, God touches his most faithful servant with unbelievable suffering and pain. For nothing that Job has done, for no sin he has committed, God visits upon him excruciating pain. As one of the saints is said to have remarked when she was wracked with suffering, "If you treat your friends this way, God, no wonder you have so few." Job suffers, but without denying God.

What could be worse than suffering all of this as Job does? Ah, suffering all this in the presence of others, and so along come a trio of Job's so-called friends to commiserate with him, and here we get into the heart of the mystery that the Book of Job examines: Why is there evil? Job's friends are clear on this issue: Bad things happen to people because they have done something evil. God wouldn't punish you unless you deserve it. So, Job, you have done something evil. Admit it, repent, and God will restore everything to you. Don't be so proud and arrogant. Admit your wrong-doing and God will forgive you.

But Job refuses. He knows he has not sinned and he demands an accounting from God. Come answer me like in a court of law. I will tell my side and you tell your side. We will determine who is right. Again and again he puts this challenge before God, and it is like God is afraid to respond to the challenge. Until He does. And when He does, it is not at all the answer Job or we expect. It is not a point by point rebuttal, but rather a picture of all the splendor of creation and all the majesty that is God's. In all of this there is no justification of His treatment of Job; rather, it is a statement that God is so far beyond anything Job can countenance or comprehend that He cannot even begin to answer the question of why. As said elsewhere in the Bible, God's ways are not our ways, and here God shows to Job that He is so far beyond one who can be held to some human reckoning.

This may or may not suit us as readers, but Job understands. He says, "I have done wrong. I repent in dust in ashes. I have meddled in areas I don't have any business being in and I am sorry. I accept God's ways." There is no answer here to why Job had to suffer, just as there is no satisfying answer to why terrible things are suffered by really very good people. We cry out Why in the face of cancer or accidents or pointless violence, but there is no satisfying answer given us that makes us say, Oh, ok, now I understand. There is no glib "She's in a better place now" that placates the mourner and alleviates the pain. There is simply the image of Job sitting there on the dung heap.

So God's answer to Job is no answer at all. At least not one that solves the problem of evil on the human level. There is the call to accept the wisdom of God or not. And that is what happens in life. Confronted with evil, we either accept God's will or we don't. We say we don't understand, but we still believe even though it is painful, or we say, "I believed in God until . . .".

But on another level, what other answer could be given? If God's ways could be comprehended by us, we would be greater than God.

# 26 RACISM

A number of years ago I was watching over the bedlam that passed for lunch at my high school when a student came up to me and asked about Joseph Conrad's *Heart of Darkness*. Not a usual conversation at lunch time from a student. I asked why he was interested in the book, a tough read for any age level, and he said that he was doing a report on it, but his own English teacher refused to talk about it.

He didn't, I asked, why not? He said it was racist and so didn't want to discuss it. Try Quillin, he said, he teaches it.

I was floored. I had been familiar with attacks on the book, a dense tale of European plundering of Africa in the colonial period. Chinwe Achebe, the great African writer, has done deeply insightful essay on the implicit racism of the novelette, which I would not attempt to refute. But the point of the criticism is that it assumes that Africa is the Dark Continent simply because it is viewed from a purely Euro-centric viewpoint that assumes other cultures have little to add.

Granted that all of that is true, the conclusion isn't to not read it. It is not helpful to race consciousness to avoid all mention of the history of literature that is racist. It is better to read something flawed that at least deals with the topic than to avoid it altogether.

Reading Jane Austen, for example, does help with a person's ability to understand different points of view and social groups, and so in that way fosters racial understanding, but that is a remote process and doesn't really bring about the kind of discussion that deals directly with race and with the views of whites and other groups toward each other. Teaching a book like *To Kill a Mockingbird* is a very different experience in a school 95% white versus teaching the same book in an inner city school that is about 95% black.

I dislike the term PC because in general it is used as a reason to never talk with any kind of sensitivity about important topics. Oh, we shouldn't say that! Someone will be offended.

Well, of course. Who likes to be referred to in hateful, hurtful terms? In that case, of course, PC is a good thing, but what has happened is that the fear of being called insensitive or worse inhibits any discussion at all. I dislike when white liberals who live in all-white sections with jobs that intersect with very few other groups condemn the racially insensitive language of less educated whites displaying their prejudices about living with blacks and other minorities.

The fault here, I think, is that these PC whites fail to see their own prejudices evident in their life choices and deftly camouflaged through urbane language. If we can never see and talk about those prejudices, there will not be much change in the area of racial equality. The teacher who sent the student to me to learn about *Heart of Darkness* could not begin to confront his own racism.

In Seattle I live in a mostly white area. That is a truism to me. Most sections of Seattle seem mostly white. I used to live in Milwaukee, a city usually at the top of the charts in terms of racially segregated cities, and yet day to day, perhaps because of the part of the city I lived in, I interacted with many more persons of color than I seem to in Seattle. But I have encountered, walking about in a mostly white area of Seattle, even in gated enclaves of Seattle, signs in the window saying "Black lives matter." And "All are welcome in this house." And yet, how easy is it to claim that all are welcome when you are living in an area where the average house is around $750,000?

I am not condemning the people who put up those signs, it's just that you have to realize the limitation of your commitment, just as you have to realize that if you never talk about race, you can't really alter or change your views or other people's views on the subject. Teaching a book that gives an out-dated or just plain wrong view of African or African-Americans can lead to a more fruitful experience than not touching upon the subject at all.

I think that in this country we have become so paranoid about saying the wrong thing that most people simply avoid the topic altogether. We have to find a way to provide a tolerant enough of an atmosphere that people say what they really think in order to ever hope to change those views.

# 27 A NOVICE PRAYER

A person who starts out in a religious order is known as a novice. This designation is meant to be temporary, as she becomes more knowledgeable about the intricacies of spirituality and religious life, she sheds the label novice for more accomplished-sounding titles. But I have always liked the image of being a novice, possibly because in a number of different areas of life I have never progressed beyond the stage of novice. I have been in more beginner yoga classes, for example, than whole ashrams full of grizzled veterans. I have been a tyro in fitness and conditioning programs all across America. Whenever I choose to brush up on language skills, I find myself enrolled in French or Spanish or Italian 101. It's that 101 label that distinguishes the true novice: there is no experience required. There seems to be many areas of life where I function as a novice, but I say that without any shame. It's nice to be a maven, an expert sharing your knowledge with the populace, but there is something very life-giving and exhilarating about embarking upon a new adventure, setting off to explore new territory. That is the life of a novice. Because there are no expectations, there is no pressure to reach a certain level of achieve a specific skill; you are just immersed in the new medium and allowed to luxuriate in it like a warm bath. You're striving ahead, Excelsior! You're simply being.

The novice is a good symbol for a way to be in the spiritual life. We can overwhelm ourselves with expectations of sanctity, feeling that after so many years of trying, we should be a whole lot better Christians than we are. Just being novices absolves us of these unreal expectations and allows us to be just bumbling followers of the Lord. It took the apostles a pretty long time to get it right in terms of what it meant to be People of the Way, and I'm not sure all of them ever got it. So with us, the path forward in the spiritual life involves frequent steps backward and sideways. If we are only novices, then that is all right; if we see ourselves as pros, then such failings are unacceptable.

The apostles were novices as they followed Jesus. A more clueless lot you probably could not find in the history of spirituality during the time of Jesus' ministry. It is only after Pentecost that they seem in any way to understand the nature of their mission and get to work. Up until that moment they seem to have witnessed most events with a slack-jawed awe.

The characteristics of a novice are: Enthusiasm, Energy, Openness, Regeneration, Optimism.

The novice approaches her new study with boundless energy and enthusiasm. She has embarked on a whole new adventure that will open up a fresh way of looking at life. Nothing captures that experience better than the "101" courses on the syllabus. Cracking open the survey volume fresh from the campus bookstore epitomizes the beginning of the search for wisdom and understanding better than anything for me. Chemistry, economics, French, anthropology -- all of these subjects promise to immerse the individual in wonderful new worlds brimming with insight and facts and new vistas of meaning.

It is hard to hang onto that optimism that characterizes the novice as we progress through life. The 101 courses devolve into long lectures, seemingly pointless assignments, and arduous exams that don't coincide with that jejune image of the first week of school. The fervor of the novice degrades into the pessimism of the plodder. We try, but cannot maintain that fresh outlook on life. It is the dynamic that characterizes so many campaigns in different aspects of life: diet, exercise, language acquisition, new skills. We desire to stay fresh and vital, but find ourselves growing stale and bitter, echoing Quoeleth that there is nothing new under the sun, why bother.

The novice in us refuses to accept this pessimism. It proclaims that there are thousands of paths out there waiting for us to explore. It eagerly responds to Jesus' invitation, "Come and see." The novice in us enthusiastically leaps at the chance to learn something challenging and new. Even the word enthusiasm, Greek for God (Theos) in (en) us speaks of the new dimension that the novice enters when she embarks on this journey.

The Gospels call us to be novices, to give up the areas where we think of ourselves as experts, safely ensconced on the departmental chairs we have established (even if it's only a Lazy-Boy), and go and seek new wisdom, new understanding. Matthew might have been an expert tax-collector, but Jesus invited him to become a novice apostle. And Matthew accepts this new vocation. Like Matthew we thrill to set foot on a new path, to follow e.e. cummings' advice: "Go for it, there's a great universe out there!"

# 28 ANXIETY

When I was younger and faced with an important life decision on what I wanted to do with my life, I found myself almost paralyzed about making a decision. I could not make a decision. I saw good in each of the paths before me, and could not find a method to come to a clear choice. My father, having grown up on a farm in the Midwest, compared my situation to that of a donkey midway between two bales of hay. Unable to decide, he eventually starved to death. As you can imagine, the simile did not amuse me, nor do I think it did much to clarify the situation. Although now I find the analogy quite amusing, I did not appreciate my father's homespun humor at the time. And yet I have to admit that the experience of being stuck in the middle does after a while resemble a life or death dilemma.

Probably the greatest realization I gleaned from this experience is how devastating decision-making can be. A great deal of the anxiety we experience in modern life comes from the many decisions we are faced with: major, life-changing ones and smaller, seemingly inconsequential ones. All of them in one way or another put pressure on us and increase the level of anxiety we deal with every day.

Paramount among the worries is the fear of making the wrong choice. The underlying script in this experience is the belief that God is holding a script of your life in front of him and watching as you veer off course and start ad-libbing instead of cleaving to the plan of the Author. Making a decision in this scenario involves guessing what God has written down for me. I think this might be what Ignatius was working off when he talked about discernment of God's will. In my prayer I would try to discern what God is calling me to do in this moment, that is, reading the text of the play he has scripted for me. Once I discern what that script is telling me to do, I have a clear path in front of me: I proceed to act out the role God has ordained for me. I hope I am not oversimplifying the essence of Ignatius' concept.

The problem with discernment for me is that it has never worked. I can picture God directing me one way and feel confident. Then again . . . After a while I can see God directing me toward the other path and I feel peace in that decision too. Which is right? Ignatius of course has provided guides for me to discern between the spirits calling me in each direction. In spite of it all, and I am more than willing to take the blame for the failure, I have not found this process a huge help in my decision making. I remain an extremely poor decision maker. I am a second-guesser, I suffer from buyer's remorse, I see the flaws in whatever choice I have made and the advantages of the path I did not go down. I am a mess.

The old saying goes, Want to make God laugh? Tell him you have a plan. In my experience this has been very true. The number of times I have had everything scoped out and in order, something has come along to upset the perfect balance and throw everything out of whack. You plan and save for a remodel of the kitchen and one of the kids needs braces or the car falls apart or someone you love just needs a hand. Something comes along that changes everything. God's hand rearranges our priorities right before our eyes. Donna Reed and Jimmy Stewart in It's a Wonderful Life are always saving for their dream, and yet something just keeps cropping up that thwarts those plans.

But the interruptions are life-giving. They don't destroy life, only our conception of what life should be. In place of that the interruptions provide a newer, richer vision of life leading to rewards and happiness we couldn't have imagined on our own. God knows what we want better than we do. Our prayers are not always answered on our terms, but they are answered to our benefit.

Decisions in our lives are the real stress causers. We fear that each decision is irreversible, immutable, and catastrophic in its consequences. But the reality is that decisions are provisional, temporary, leading in directions that change with the weather, move into terrain we did not envision, and yet we flourish once we surrender to this change and revision. We find that the decision we made doesn't last, can't be acted on, must be revised, or leads to disaster. And yet the new direction, the new road, brings unplanned richness and joy.

From my experience of teaching high school kids who are going through the throes of making decisions about colleges and life goals, I know that I am not alone. Many of us experience deep anxiety about decisions we have to make in our lives. Here is what I have learned about the issue so far.

First, I don't like the idea that there is a script for me that I must learn and anticipate. I do not think that there is one path already sketched out for us to travel along, but rather a network of possibilities, each one leading to others and others so that we can make our way according to our own lights. Each choice leads to others. The process of making a choice, then, should not be hampered entirely by the fear of making the wrong decision, but of choosing the one that is more life-giving. If we fail to choose that one, though, it is not that we are mired for all eternity on the wrong track. Decisions are for the most part reversible. It may come at a cost, but bad decisions can be undone and new ones made. As I would tell my students, choosing a college that turns out to be a bad match for you will certainly lead to more problems and work than making a better choice right off, but your poor choice does not mean your life is ruined. There are ways of undoing that choice, picking up the pieces and moving forward. In some ways, that wrong choice will give you insight that might prevent an unwise choice in the future.

So the anxiety a student feels as she makes a choice for college is understandable, but she must also be aware that any choice is going to bring her wisdom and knowledge and prepare her for future choices. Even choosing the less felicitous option adds to her experience, and as someone once said, experience is a good teacher. That person added that it was also a hard one, but some of us can't take it as truth when told that the stove is hot, we have to touch it ourselves. The student choosing unwisely leaves herself with more work to do, but not in a pit she can't climb out of.

That may not seem like a lot of consolation, but I think it is important to realize that many decisions in life are reversible. They are not reversed without a certain amount of pain and effort, and they will leave scars, but they are reversible. God's plan for us is more open-ended than we tend to conceive it to be. God's plan for each of us, I believe, has an element of fuzziness about it too. God sees us, since He gave us free will, as capable of moving in many different directions. More like the queen on a chessboard than a pawn, but with the added ability to go off the grid altogether and strike out on our own. Such knowledge should give us hope and power rather than imprison us in doubt and insecurity.

# 29 LOVE

I had a chapter on faith and hope, so it made sense to include a chapter on love, but I almost didn't include this chapter because so much has already been said on this topic. So much good and bad that it is difficult to think that I could add anything to this discussion. And yet it is so central that I can't pass by without even a nod in its general vicinity.

However, I will spare you my feeble attempt at defining love. That has been done so many other places so much better than I could possibly do it, and believe me, that is not false modesty on my part, just a statement of fact. What I will talk about is our response to love. I will take as a given that you have experienced love in your life either by its presence or its absence and in some way have come to your own understanding of the term, but what is your response to this love?

There is a point early in the Mass where it is asked," What return shall I make for all that the Lord has given me?" And the response is that I will take the cup of salvation and call upon His name. Ignatius talks about seeing all of creation as an expression of God's love for us and asks what response shall we make.

The response to this love is to live. God's great love for us calls us to live as fully and lavishly as we can a life of love in response. We are not to be timid, to cower in fear, to secrete away our talents like the fearful servant, but to be bold in living a life of faith and generosity, walking the earth performing miracles, large and small. True life, lived in fullness, is our expression of thanks to God for all He has given us.

How you view love is how you live your life. If you have a low, mean view of what love has been in your life, you will not have any love to share with others. If you are overwhelmed with the abundance of love God has showered on you, you will not hesitate to shower that same love on others. You cannot dwell in the darkness of despair and hate when you are conscious of the great shining love God has given to you.

There is a pop song that has the line "You were better to me than I was to myself." I love that line. I suspect the rest of the song speaks of pretty mundane things, but that line sticks out to me with a great expression of the effects of God's love. God's love treats us much much better than we treat ourselves. It is full and generous, it does not judge us or condemn us. It does, in fact, do all of those things that Paul talks about to the Corinthians about the nature of love. It ultimately endures. It remains, securely, locked in our souls.

And our response should be the same. We are kind, and patient. We are patient and kind, we are not jealous or self-important, we don't judge or rejoice in someone's misfortunes. We bear all things, we believe all things, we hope all things, and we endure in our love because we have been first and most fully loved by God.

# 30 HYPOCRISY

The age we are in says there is only one sin left standing: hypocrisy. In any movie or TV show the villain is instantly recognized: he is the person who takes the high moral ground. Inevitably, that person who espouses some clearly delineated moral stance at the start of the drama will be de-pantsed figuratively if not literally before the show is over. And while such moral comeuppance is satisfying enough from the time of the Romans Plautus and Terence to Shakespeare and on, there comes a point where we wonder, Fair enough, but what do you have in place of that? Of course the foppish Duke deserves what he gets, but what about the rest? Is there something left standing? Or is the only remaining value to have no value? To be tolerant of everything and nothing at the same time?

But when is an attack on hypocrisy nothing more than an empty statement? When do you progress beyond attacking hypocrisy and declare what you do stand for? Is every proponent of a moral code an empty poseur? Does every believer secretly subvert his own creed? Are we then at heart only vile creatures with just a few representatives honest enough to admit that they are vile? This is the image that emerges from a satire without any alternatives. Every espousal of faith is bound by definition to be exposed and ridiculed as a vapid display of duplicity.

The modern picture of the evangelist caught in some illicit tryst or crusading politician caught with his fingers in the till is a commonplace of journalism today. The recent lists of priests who have been identified as sexual predators is an especially sad and cruel statement of just how terribly corrupt supposedly virtuous human beings can become. It's hardly news; it's dog bites man. Real news, ironically, has become a story where the evangelist is actually a good guy or the politician who really was interested in righting wrongs.

The fear of hypocrisy has become so overwhelming that many people are fearful of doing or saying anything that would put them in a position where they might be subject to those attacks on their integrity. Who among us if he or she is honest, does not see points in their lives where they have been unfaithful to their ideals? Not necessarily in the sense of living a life of lies, but simply in the sense of having slipped from what they had hoped to be their better selves? Yet, if frailty and culpability are obstacles that eliminate us from ever speaking out on our beliefs, then all that remain are those fatuous and oblivious enough to see no errors in their lives -- exactly those most prone to hypocrisy. Our own faults cannot keep us from sharing what we truly believe and what we want to pass down to our children and beyond. In spite of our weaknesses, we say, this is what we believe, what we stand for.

The example of the disciples is a good guide for us in this matter. They were not sinless, perfect creatures. They misunderstood, they feared, fought over who should be most important, but they still followed. And Jesus loved them. He understood who they were and he still desired that they go forth and preach his message. In the same way, Jesus does not desire that our own sins prevent us from proclaiming his message to the world through words and actions. His injunction to carry his message to all of the world is meant for us, and we need to heed it even if it puts us in the uneasy position of being a target for others.

# 31 ABORTION

I was out with my wife and some of her friends when the subject of abortion came up. One of the party, a woman of strong convictions who had had a career in art, said as if stating an irrefutable fact: Well, if a person doesn't like abortion, don't have one. I was quite surprised by this, since I had always thought of this woman as a perceptive intellectual and yet how could she have settled for such a facile cliche? Where could this heinous piece of reasoning not be used? Well, if you don't like assault rifles, don't buy one. Well, if you don't like child pornography, don't look at it. Or animal cruelty or sex slavery, and on and on.

And yet the statement sat out there, unchallenged. A group of intellectually shrewd individuals failed to challenge the thesis at all. In other areas rigorously demanding, this group here all tacitly acquiesced, which shows I think the state to which the "debate" if we can call it that, has sunk in the area of abortion. On both sides of the issue pat adages and slogans have replaced any kind of real exchange on the topic. At this point, it seems that almost no one is still looking for insight and enlightenment on the topic; everyone has made up his or her mind.

So can anything further be said about the issue or are we doomed to a trench warfare where the two sides slog through the months and years with fatalities but no progress made? Can we never reach any kind of a rapprochement where the two sides find some agreement that is at least partially palatable to both parties? The issue is no longer one issue among many, but rather the litmus test that decides allegiances and elections to the exclusion of other equally vital issues. The great failing of the Democratic Party of late is their failure to recognize how key this issue is, not just to the radical right, but to many caring, compassionate individuals who cannot see their way clear to vote for a candidate who espouses the right to abortion in any situation.

In an area where any hint of compromise is seen as betrayal and worse, I think it is essential to find a way forward that acknowledges the rights of both sides while probably also angering both sides. I think there is a fair amount of fuzzy faith necessary to proceed through this slough, but here goes my simplified answer.

Give three months on each side. Allowing an abortion through the first three months acknowledges the rights of a woman to determine the course of her own body and life. It also says that the debate of when life begins is at least open still to some definitive formulation. To not allow an abortion during the last three months might in some ways curtail the woman's total control over her body, but in so many areas of life one right is conditioned by other rights and demands. The measure also acknowledges the very real biological truth that by this point the fetus is by all intents and purposes a viable human being, regardless of at what point she or he became so. Anyone who has witnessed an intensive care unit for premature babies is aware of how fully human these babies are at the six month point.

What about the middle months? Well, that's where debates and individual regions will have to iron out some sort of agreement, but at least there is somewhere to have as a starting point to work things out.

So, both sides are probably mad at this point, but I maintain that something has been gained by each side. Clearly, for the moral absolutist such a bargain is reprehensible and heinous, but it is a way forward. Am I open to condemnation by those occupying the moral high ground on both sides? Absolutely (no pun). But this does not seem an issue that can be decided by the absolutists.

There's a whole debate here about moral principles and

whether we can compromise when we are dealing with matters that involve such principles. It is a complicated one, and perhaps my approach is too simplistic, but it seems that some way forward through this impasse is called for. If some capitulation does not occur on each side, the issue will be decided, not by the stronger moral position, but solely by the side in power. Not to me a salubrious solution.

# 32 O.T. GOD

One of the concepts modern theology has succeeded in drumming into the minds of students is the difference between the Old Testament God and the New Testament God. The difference, most products of a grade school set of theology courses will tell you, is that the Old Testament portrays a severe God quick with the thunderbolts and lightning, while the New Testament presents us with a loving, forgiving God.

The only problem with that facile distinction is that it's not very accurate. In fact, my reaction after having tripped lightly through the Old Testament, taking as much as the patience of teenagers will allow is quite different. The prevailing image that I come away with is of a rather befuddled God who doesn't think things through all that well. He seems almost a fit topic for a sitcom than the God of all history.

In order to explain, let me start with a term that you probably already know, in which case you can skip this paragraph. Anthropomorphism is the practice of portraying someone or thing (in this case God) who is not human in human terms. Showing a rabbit as a wisecracking fellow who has a fondness for practical jokes is giving a nonhuman animal human characteristics. Similarly, if we show God as a person who gets angry, seeks revenge, or wants to destroy His creation like a petulant child knocking over his Lego project, we give God our own human characteristics.

Anthropomorphism is understandable in terms of God, because God is beyond our understanding. We cannot comprehend God; if we could, we would be God's equal. The Old Testament figures understood that when they banned any illustrations of God or even of saying his name. How, then, can you say anything at all about God? Well, you can't. Not if you're being completely accurate. The minute you start to talk about God, you limit Him. Even saying "him" puts on God gender, which is inaccurate -- another reason why using the masculine or feminine pronoun, he or she, is equally inaccurate. Once you give God human characteristics you are putting limits on God that are not there, not if God is an infinite, unlimited creature. But we need to talk about God, so we make a deal: we say we are going to use human terms, but you have to understand that this is no more than an analogy, an approximation that is meant to illustrate a truth, but not be the truth itself.

So, when the Old Testament writer sat down to talk about God, he used terms he understood. When reading the Old Testament, you find a number of different models that they fell back on: an angry leader, a forgiving one, a maker or creator, a shepherd, etc. According to the writer, each figure emphasized different strengths of God, but always the underlying agreement was that God was more than what could be set down on paper or parchment. The image that I see frequently in the Old Testament is of a God who is easily cozened. With Noah and Lot and Moses, God is someone who is quick to anger. He looks around and sees sin and evil everywhere and says He will destroy the lot, pun accepted. He will drown the earth, bring fire, destroy the cities. Then someone must counsel prudence and talk God out of his funk. Lot says, well what if I can find 50 faithful people, will you spare all of them? And God agrees. And agrees again and again as Lot bargains him down like a dealer at a cheap open air market. God here is clearly presented in anthropomorphic terms and not even in the best of human terms. He is childish in his pique, short-sighted in terms of the consequences and, let's face it, not very bright. Cooler heads than God must prevail so that humanity can continue to exist.

Reread some of those stories. They don't present the most impressive image of God that we have. We're a little embarrassed by the pictures, in fact. So, what conclusion can we draw from these images? Are they just early sketches that are best forgotten?

# 33 INDIFFERENCE

In his First Principle and Foundation, Ignatius is very explicit: He is indifferent about whether God sends him good experiences or bad, sickness or health, wealth or poverty. Yes, that is true, but he also says that if all other things are equal, he would rather choose suffering and poverty because that puts him more in line with what Jesus suffered.

Some say we have to understand St. Ignatius' concept of indifference in context. He didn't want suffering, he was simply willing to bear it. But I don't think that is true. Ignatius' wording in his Foundation is quite explicit and unambiguous (I looked it up!):

"Consequently, as far as we are concerned, we should not prefer health to sickness, riches to poverty, honor to dishonor, a long life to a short life. The same holds for all other things.

Our one desire and choice should be what is more conducive to the end for which we are created."

The meaning, it seems to me, is painfully clear: nothing in creation should appeal to us more than its opposite; the only thing that matters is doing the will of God. Along with loving your enemies, I believe this is the hardest stricture Christianity lays upon us. Who can do this? It's human nature to want to survive and thrive, to prosper and not wither. Who wouldn't want that? Who sees a gravely ill person in the hospital and says, "Oh, I want that"? Who says, "A lot of money or living on the street? I don't care, it's the same to me."

And yet that is what Ignatius is saying and what he lived. There was a point in his life where the whole Society of Jesus, the order he had worked so long and hard to establish, was on the brink of dissolving, of failure. And Ignatius' attitude was that if that was the will of God, then so be it. Everything gone in an instant? It's OK.

As strong as this statement is, it pales in comparison to what Ignatius says when he discusses his Third Degree of Humility. In the words of one online translation (again, I looked it up) he states:

"The third is most perfect Humility; namely, when -- including the first and second, and the praise and glory of the Divine Majesty being equal -- in order to imitate and be more actually like Christ our Lord, I want and choose poverty with Christ poor rather than riches, opprobrium with Christ replete with it rather than honors; and to desire to be rated as worthless and a fool for Christ, Who first was held as such, rather than wise or prudent in this world."

What sane person would want this?

There is no way of defending Ignatius' point of view through ordinary worldly wisdom, nothing in what he says resonates with most of us, even if we are truly seeking the good. It goes against every instinct of self-preservation. How can you possibly wish ill toward yourself? I can't. I don't even know if I wish I could. Sort of looking at those body-building people, would you even want that many muscles if you had the discipline to develop them? I wouldn't. All right, maybe it's not like that at all, but you get my drift, don't you?

I will give you another absurd example. One saint, I think it was Theresa of Avila, once said that if it could lessen the suffering of Jesus one second, she would gladly choose hell, separation from God for all eternity. Think about it. Here was a woman driven by fierce belief. Heaven and hell weren't just concepts, but stark, undeniable realities. And Jesus? He was a living, vibrant person Theresa ardently followed. And to be separated for all eternity from this love? Not a problem if it could make the suffering of Jesus even one second shorter.

Again, incomprehensible!

Two great mystics, John of the Cross and Mother Teresa

spent years in unutterable darkness, praying and yet receiving no consolation, no validation of their efforts. God, they believed, was there but he resolutely refused to make his presence known to two of his most faithful followers. How was that possible for them to continue to believe, to continue to pray? I haven't a clue. If anyone lived a life embodying Ignatius's ideal of the Third Degree of Indifference, these two saints did. How they could maintain their fierce love and loyalty to God through all of that is beyond me.

There is a level where faith is not the good sense, nice-to-have-along panacea we like to make it into. Sometimes true, deep faith makes no earthly sense. It's not the "best policy" or the way to succeed in the world like Ben Franklin's Virtues. Faith at times just gets in the way of our own best interests and leads us away from self-preservation into the dark alleys of fearful allegiances and passions. It leads in directions that have nothing to do with smiley faced mottoes printed on acid-free paper or banners to be strung in windows and auditoriums. This kind of faith is an embarrassing, disreputable invasion into the quiet suburban avenues of proper Sunday morning practice. That is the purlieu of The Third Degree of Indifference. It is the spokesperson we want to keep off stage during the fund drive or the new member recruitment sessions. "Shhh, wait, wait until they join before you hit them with those things. They don't want to hear that now."

I'm not sure what part this third level plays in the daily life of Christians. Surely we are not all called to exhibit it (I hope.) We can aspire to it. I myself pray for the courage to want to pray for it, which if you stop to think about it is pretty far down the line to getting it. But it's the most I can see myself wanting at the moment.

Self-preservation on the physical level is so strong in our makeup. How could we who believe in another, more important spiritual dimension possibly wish for bad things to happen to us? How many kids do you run into named Job? Me? Not a lot, and I think with good reason. In spite of the wisdom he ends up with, what parent would wish that life on her child?

How do I apply these passionate interpretations of Christianity in my own life? I don't think I do. At this point all I can do is to pray to one day have that much faith, that much generosity of spirit. But for the moment, I still fear death and sickness, I still want a comfortable life like I have at the moment as I sit warm looking out at the cold Seattle rain rather than huddling under a viaduct somewhere downtown, trying to get out of the wind and stay dry.

I still want you to read this book and think I'm quite the guy rather than laughing at it and saying what a shallow and vapid individual that Quillin must be. I'm sorry, I don't want those things to be important, but they continue to be. I would rather have friends than be ridiculed and mocked, be healthy rather than languishing in a hospital somewhere. I want to say none of these things matter as long as I am serving God, but I know how false such a statement is at this point.

All I can do is to pray for this depth of faith at some time.

# 34 SELF-DOUBT

Wait! Don't skip this chapter! This is not another of those positive thinking pitches to get you to abandon your years of self-doubt in favor of a full speed ahead, no hesitation plunge into the future. This chapter is meant as a praise of self-doubt.

Just as I am aware of the many pitfalls of self-doubt, how it sometimes paralyzes us and keeps us from fully using our potential, there is also a kind comforting side to self-doubt. It is a characteristic that makes us aware that there are other people out there, other points of view, other solutions to problems. Just as "plagued with self-doubt" can be criticism, so can the designation of a man as "not being cursed with self-doubt." It suggests a man who plunges forward convinced of his own superior knowledge and insight, having no need of consultation or collegiality. Up against such a figure the person of self-doubt does not seem an entirely bad option.

Self-doubt, then, at its best (if such a thing can have a best) functions as a self-examination in the light of other people's views. It becomes a mini-examen helping us to gauge how what we are doing will affect and be received by others. It's the look before you leap syndrome where you exercise caution about what you are preparing to do. Will your actions hurt those around you? Will they do what you intend or cause more harm than good? These are questions of a person concerned with the larger world around her rather than simply her own feelings and ambitions.

In such a manner self-doubt helps us to achieve that paradox that is at the heart of the Gospels and expressed so beautifully in the prayer of St. Francis:

"O Divine Master, grant that I may not so much seek to be consoled as to console; to be understood as to understand; to be loved as to love. For it is in giving that we receive; it is in pardoning that we are pardoned; and it is in dying that we are born to eternal life."

Our first impulse, to cater to our own needs, isn't the one that we heed. A moment of hesitation, or self-doubt, brings a deeper, richer alternative. Our happiness, as important as it is to us, takes second place to the happiness of others, and in doing that, Surprise!, our own happiness is paradoxically greater.

That is the heart of the benefits of self-doubt. Like most sharp instruments, wielded carelessly it can do more harm than good, but carefully applied, it is an effective brake on those moments when we are certain that we have all of the answers and there really isn't any need for listening to others or looking at the situation from another point of view.

So charge ahead, O you of self-doubt. Excelsior! To the top! But be careful of those flowers there and don't trod on any bunnies.

# 35 THANKFULNESS

If the great challenges to the spiritual life are fear and envy, the antidote to these is thankfulness. Thankfulness stands as the great virtue of the modern age. It does so much for us and for other people. I think it is the main way we imitate Jesus. Thankfulness doesn't stand out as the paramount virtue of Jesus' life, and yet it must have been his constant attitude toward all he saw and did. It is thankfulness for the Father's gift of life he celebrates in healing the sick, raising up the lowly, feeding the hungry. As if to say, I will use these wonderful gifts I have received from the Father to glorify and magnify his presence on earth.

We can't be truly grateful and still be bitter or envious or unhappy. There is just something in the nature of thankfulness that crowds out those other negative emotions. See someone else who has something nice? If you are thankful for what you have, you will be happy that that person has something nice too. If you are miserable and unsatisfied, you will be envious of the other person. Think of someone you know who is truly a thankful person. (If you can't think of anyone, it's time to go out and make some new friends.) Note how she responds to you and to the world around her. She is much less likely to need to talk about herself and what she has accomplished. She is more open to hearing about you, because she is secure and contented in her own life. There is a positive energy that flows out from her own sense of thankfulness and peace.

Here's an exercise you have been asked to do many times. I hate when a book asks me to do an exercise. I think it's a way of the author just making me do his work. If you think that now, you're probably right. But do it anyway, because no matter how many times you are asked to do this, it's not enough. And the other great thing about it is that each time you do it, your answers change.

Name five things you are truly grateful for in your life right now:

1.

2.

3
.

4.

5.


What do you do when you give thanks for something? Ah, there's a question you might not have been asked before! I might not be quite as hackneyed as you thought! What do you do? What does it mean to give thanks? Do you say, Thank you, Jesus? Do you say, I hope I remember the next time I see my friend I say to her Thanks for being my friend. Am I more aware as I use or experience that thing, that I am thankful for it?

In a word, does your thankfulness lead to any change or action on your part? It can, of course, simply be a momentary experience, thanks for this. But it can also be a deeper part of our lives. Being thankful for this leads me to want to do this or to be this way or to have this attitude in the future. In this way thankfulness becomes a way of ordering our lives, providing a goal and a standard for living. Do I celebrate my thankfulness for God's life by the way I act in my daily life?

# 36 SEXUALITY

I was part of a team who were addressing seniors before their prom. We had all of the usual talks about the dangers of driving and alcohol. There was a policeman who spoke about the horrific crashes he had seen in his years on the force. That year I think we even had a car towed onto the parking lot that had been crashed in a high-speed accident. As the stock saying goes, alcohol was involved. I do not know if there were any fatalities from that particular crash, but from the look of the car, I would not have been surprised.

Such demonstrations are necessary these days because of the awful consequences of drinking and driving, but I was struck by the fact that nobody was willing to talk about the other elephant in the room. Many of these students were going to parties after the prom that involved renting hotel rooms for the night and getting in as much alcohol as possible. At that particular point the danger was less drinking and driving than drinking and sex. The pressure to engage in sex during such an evening is intense, and yet no one was talking about the importance of decisions made on that night. I find in general that that assembly was a microcosm of society in general. For the most part we older adults are not comfortable talking about sex with younger people in our care. One parent explained to me one time that fathers were not at ease talking about alcohol and sex with their children because they had such a poor record in those areas themselves. As one father put it, it was hard to preach to his children without feeling like a hypocrite himself.

I think that this is a result of hearing years of horror stories when we were young of couples killed while making out in a car parked on the train tracks. Why they chose train tracks for the rendezvous I never understood, but the point was made that sex led to catastrophic consequences. We've moved beyond those stories certainly, but haven't really replaced them with ones more accessible to a new generation. What do we say to younger people whose sexual experience has proceeded at a pace unheard of in the previous generation? My sophomore students have faced many more difficult decisions in the area of sexuality than I did by the time I was out of college. Add to this the tremendous impact delivered by media such as movies, Internet, and television, and you have a world far beyond anything imaginable a generation or two back. And yet they seem to get much less advice and feedback.

There are many reasons for this paucity of preaching. The feeling of inadequacy mentioned above plays a role in it. As mentioned earlier, there is also the failure brought on by the scandals among the clergy which weakened everyone's resolve to speak up on this issue. Who wants to set himself or herself up as the moral spokesperson in an area so fraught with pitfalls? And yet it would seem imperative to say something even if it only bounces around in the canyon and boomerangs back to us in empty echoes. So here goes.

A major challenge in the modern age of sexual maturity is the split between fantasy and reality. The fantasy side of life is so much more powerful and compelling than it once was. I had a friend in one of the major tech companies tell me that the money and drive to develop new virtual reality technology was the porn industry. His observation is borne out by the proliferation of VR internet sites and software programs. Directed primarily at younger male audiences, such games and reality programs foster values that bring out some of the worst of the male impulses. The situations and responses take fantasy to the edge at least of reality.

Our weapons against such a process seem weak and limited indeed, but at least we need to make the effort to point out that such fantasies lead not to happiness, but to an anodyne substitute for values like maturity, love, compassion. We need to encourage a clear understanding that such realities where we control the environment are not the same as the real world where we interact and connect to other centers of feelings, emotions, and dreams. The talk about sex today maybe has less to do with a catalog of prescribed and proscribed actions and more to do with the underlying attitudes toward life and reality and what we believe constitutes happiness for us and others.

In the famous Deuteronomy text, God enjoins the Israelites to choose life. Today's world screams the same message: Choose life with all of its complications over the fantasy world offered where we are always at the center, always in control. No one may be comfortable about sexuality to fearlessly guide others, but many realize that ins and outs, ups and downs of contending with this major part of our existence defines who we are and indeed forms us in the very core of our being.

# 37 SACRAMENTS

The hardest religious topic to talk about and not be boring is the Sacraments. I never found any religion teacher who clamored to have the section on Sacraments. It's an important topic, but just tends to be a snoozer for some reason. With that in mind, I won't be offended if you skip this chapter, but I think you should hang around and read it.

My definition of sacraments: They are the rituals that bind us together as a family. The term family is thrown around a great deal, but belonging to the Church is meaningless if it doesn't include being part of a family, and the sacraments are our way of celebrating that kinship. Baptism welcomes us into the family, the Eucharist is that meal that nourishes our membership, Confirmation acknowledges our maturity in that family, and Reconciliation is our way of turning back to our family after wandering or running away. They mark the milestones of our lives as Christians. We are born into an open, loving family that is the opposite of some elite, exclusive club; we belong and from this solid foundation we reach out to embrace others into this love.

Sacraments are the icons of our life of faith. Like the cross itself, sacraments are the intersection of the horizontal and vertical, the earthly and divine. They are the signs that we participate in something greater than the visible life we see here. We are, by Baptism, born into a family; by Communion we share in a feast of God's love, and by Confirmation we accept a role of responsibility for growing in this relationship and sharing God's love with all.

Our birth into a family of God forms the basis for all of

our morality. If we do not share this kinship with those around us, why treat all people with love and fairness? We recognize them as sisters and brothers who share (whether acknowledged or not) the same heavenly Father, and so we take care of them. We suffer when they suffer, experience joy and triumph when they do. Baptism is the symbol of our entrance into, not a society of the saved, but into a rather disreputable mongrel family of many members, not all salubrious. In short, we live in union with all, and Baptism is our sign of that unity.

Communion is the meal that celebrates our acceptance into this family -- deserved or not. We sit down at the table of the Lord, not because we have done anything meritorious to earn this meal, but because by Baptism we have been freely accepted into it. We come together much as the misbehaving youngster is accepted to the dinner table because already it is known that the child is forgiven.

And that forgiveness is most especially marked by the sacrament of Penance or Confession. Penance says that mistakes are not permanent, that forgiveness prevails. Even though our response to love at times is a turning away toward drugs, diversions, and avoidance, God is always waiting. In that beautiful play, I Never Sang for My Father, the main character, who is haunted by the missed opportunities of his relationship with his father, is told: "Death doesn't end a relationship, it merely changes it." We can reject the relationship with God, but that doesn't end it. God is still there and you still have a relationship with God, even if it's only one of denial at the moment. Penance says that denial isn't the final word. Loving union is still available. We can even hide in the old dodge that I am not worthy, but God is still there saying, Of course, you're not worthy; no one is. But nevertheless you are still loved by me.

Confirmation is the signal that you are an adult ready to take responsibility for the family, to be Disciples. As St. Ignatius stresses always, real Love is shown in deeds more than in words. Confirmation calls us to begin doing those deeds. One of my favorite gospel stories is the parable of the two brothers who are

131

asked by the father to go out in the fields and do some work for him. The one is annoyed and says he won't; the other brother smiles and tells the father that of course we will gladly do it. But later, the first brother gets feeling bad about not going and he goes out and does the work. The other brother, after agreeing, blithely forgets his promise and neglects to do his father's will. Confirmation anoints us into that band who (maybe without perfect, good will) accepts God's mission and goes out and does his will. It is a sign of maturity and decision.

It is a rejection of the second son's attitude, again another example of Bonhoffer's Cheap Grace, that glib acceptance of God is Love, but the inertia of not responding to what that love calls us to do. True grace calls on us to respond.

In Confirmation we become sacraments ourselves, signs to the world of God's love. By our actions we affirm to others the existence of God and of God's love.

# 38 REPETITION

See it's working! Let's review the key points of repetition.
What? You can't remember any?
That's why we repeat.

Right now.
Right here.
This is it.

Ignatius thought repetition was at the heart of good teaching.

# 39 CAFETERIA CATHOLICS

One of the favorite whipping boys of modern sermons is what's called the Cafeteria Catholics. These are those so-called Catholics who shop around for doctrines palatable to their tastes. Whenever they hear something harsh or distasteful, they walk away, much as many followers walked away from Jesus when he told them that unless they were willing to eat his flesh and drink his blood, they couldn't be his followers.

Put like that Cafeteria Catholicism seems a shameful thing indeed. To accept or reject the core tenets of belief solely on the basis or whether or not we feel up to living them is to gut the heart of faith, but frequently the term Cafeteria Catholics is used to describe something totally different and with that I disagree. Often preachers -- and particularly bad ones -- will use the term to disparage Catholics who move from one parish to another solely on the basis of the priest(s) in a particular parish. In the old order of things, it should not matter who the priest was, since it was the sacrament that counted. A Mass, even if offered in a monotone, uninterested manner, was still a Mass. The Mass was the essential mystery, independent of the person performing the rite.

Which is true enough, as far as it goes, but that thought about the efficacy of the sacrament fails to take in all that has come about since Vatican II. It is clear now that things like the liturgy, now said in a language most of the congregation can follow, should make an effort to engage the congregation. The message of those who disparage the Cafeteria Catholics is that you should remain at a parish even if the priest is not s person who speaks to your own position in life, but to me that doesn't make sense. We discontinue going to a doctor who no longer seems attuned to your particular needs. Obviously, if we quit a doctor just because she says we need to get exercise and that gravy isn't a suitable beverage, then we are making a mistake. But if the doctor seems preoccupied with keeping to a schedule and forgets who you are, then it probably is a good idea to find another care-giver.

The same with a parish and its priest. If the main focus of every liturgy is a long way from where you are living, then it makes sense to try somewhere else. I currently go past about three or four parishes on a Sunday to make it to mine. I have tried the other ones, at one point I even belonged to two of them, but I have since established that this current one is the parish that most nearly fits my needs. Is that being a Cafeteria Catholic? I suppose it is, but it is a sensible one. To explore the metaphor itself, one doesn't go down the lunch line meekly accepting every food item slapped onto the tray; rather, we select elements that we judge will most completely fit our present needs. The same with a parish.

To give you an example. My wife and I belonged to parish close by our home. The priest worked hard to provide thoughtful, prepared homilies. He tried to involve all elements of the parish from the grade schoolers through the senior citizens and the parish tried to reach out with apostolic missions and social programs to the wider world. It was, all in all, a good parish for us. Exit this priest; enter Father Fire, who spent his opening sermon excoriating us for not showing up for Confession on Friday. Subsequent liturgies demonstrated that this was not a one-time fixation; the focus of each week was on how we were not living the good old-time religion God had handed down to us. Now, the choice was clear: in the Church of my youth one was stuck with whatever pastor the diocese foisted upon you, but today there are more viable options. And options we took, transitioning to a parish where once again homilies focused on the message of the gospels and the outreach of the parish was toward trying to bring succor and relief to a suffering world.

Was such a change wrong? Well, maybe I should have stayed and tried to change the situation in my first parish, but I doubt that I would have had much impact there. This was not a cleric plagued with self-doubt. Should I have stayed and quietly submitted as some of the great mystics of the Church had done? Perhaps, but alas I suspect I lack that staying power. I probably would have just started finding reasons for not attending Mass on Sundays. But was I justified in switching? I think yes. In fact, I think it was important for me to change in order to keep giving my faith a chance to grow. It was better here to be a Cafeteria Catholic than a lapsed one.

# 40 THE TEST PRAYER

As a teacher one of the more monotonous tasks that she is asked to do during her career is to proctor exams, either her own or others. For a period of an hour or more, the teacher is asked to do nothing but hand out and explain a test, then watch that no untoward transmission of information takes place. Because of the need for vigilance, it's really impossible to do other things like grade papers or read a book. As with any time when one is forced to just sit there, time passes very slowly.

Perhaps to combat that boredom I developed what I call my Test Prayer. It proceeds like this. I go down the aisles. It is one of those rare opportunities to observe other people without being worried that you will be caught at it ;after all, you're supposed to be looking at them to make sure they're not cheating or anything. So I just observe them. It's amazing. They are so focused, trying hard to remember what they learned or were supposed to have learned. What was that he said? What did I write down in my notebook about that? They are concentrating so hard that they have no energy left to dissemble, to put on a certain look to the outside world, and their vulnerability makes them, each and every one of them, even the must intractable and rambuctious during ordinary classes, now so open and transparent.

And it is at moments like these that I am able to contemplate the students as individuals and not as a class. I see each of them, not as a component of the group that I must contend with each day, but as one person filled with hopes and expectations, fears and dreams, and I see them as their parents must see them as they send them off to school each day. They aren't students then, but that special son or daughter that the parents have so many hopes and fears for. And I pray for each one individually that she fulfills all of her expectations, finds that special spot in God's plan that she is not sure is even there for her. Going down the row I pray that that boy hunched over his test right now overcomes his fears, masters his many secret voices telling him he's not good enough and realizes how special he is and how much God loves him.

It is a great way for me to see each student as she is, a unique wonderful individual, not simply a member of a class. Teaching each day one is struck by individual students for good or bad reasons, but there isn't the time to savor each student as a person. During these quiet moments of a test I can do exactly that, and I find that this prayer changes how I see each student during the rest of the time too. I tend to be less liable to see them as the other, the enemy, but more as someone I'm pulling for, someone struggling to reach a goal and that I'm going to do whatever I can to help them reach it.

I recommend the test prayer. I wish I would have discovered it earlier in life. I think that if you are not a teacher there must be ways of adapting the prayer to your particular situation, maybe by looking at a roster or directory of your colleagues or the persons in your care.

# 41 WOMEN

Do you know what the situation in the Church today regarding women is like? It's like in the Renaissance when just about anyone who read a book or the equivalent at the time knew that the sun was the center of the universe. As Copernicus had demonstrated beyond refutation, the earth, with the other planets, revolved around the sun. Everyone knew that, but some in the Church felt that this truth would undermine faith itself and so required the "faithful" to cling to the notion of an earth-centered universe. So, on the one hand most thinking individuals held to the sun-centered universe and then paid lip service to a view that clashed with every rational instinct they had.

We face a similar dichotomy today. There are no real arguments out there forbidding the ordination of women, just a few shameful remnants of worn-out aphorisms about needing to grow beards to be able to perform sacramental duties. A down-on-your-luck circus trying to foist off geek shows and tired animals on a sophisticated audience that has moved on in their thinking and tastes. Not many people, I think, cling to the idea that there is any intrinsic reason forbidding the ordination of women, and most are a bit ashamed when we hear the old adages trotted out. It's a forgone conclusion, an idea whose time has come and then some. And yet we cling to the notion, much as people must have mouthed the words affirming an earth-centered universe while at the same time looking out of the corner of their eyes to see whether anyone was watching them. It is a strange trench to die in. So many more worthy causes to throw one's life upon rather than this anachronistic redoubt.

How would you go about getting women ordained? Here's a simple solution: Take every woman who is 35 or older and is a member of a recognized religious order of nuns. If she has had theological background and is willing, ordain her. Wouldn't that let in some unqualified priests? Possibly, but more so than we have already with our present system? I don't think so. This may be too drastic a solution, but isn't it clear to most people at this point in history that the Church leadership is missing some key input in terms of its reflection and direction? Doesn't the very exclusion of women from the important positions in the Church seriously handicap it in terms of understanding and responding to the modern world? We can at times compensate for this imbalance by setting up committees to better collect insights from women, but we are only doing stop-gap measures to try to remedy a wrong that no longer needs to exist.

There are practical considerations, I am sure, that would complicate the ordination of women, but these are certainly minor compared to the clear advantage of righting a long-established wrong and of moving closer toward the Church's mission to be universal than anything else we can do at this point.

It is a strange situation when you consider that most of the men in the positions of authority in the Church are good men and well meaning and yet they cannot be actively moving toward sharing this office and privilege with women. Conceding good intentions to these men, I cannot understand what the hesitation might be, and I would consider myself much more moderate than many in and out of the Church. What must such foot dragging seem like to the younger generation whose battleground has been in areas like LGBT than a centuries-old distrust of the other sex?

# 42 JONAH, HOLD THE WHALE

This is about Jonah, but it's not about the whale. The worst thing that happened to the Jonah story was the inclusion of the whale, which is the only part people remember, but it's not at all the central part. This is about that central part, and definitely NOT about a whale!

You should really sit down and read the "Book of Jonah" first before reading this chapter. Not just because it makes this chapter clearer but because it is a great little story. It's short, it won't take any time at all, and you will thoroughly enjoy it. Besides, you'll have bragging rights -- "Yup, sorry I'm a little late, I was busy just knocking off a book of the Bible." Everybody knows the part of Jonah getting swallowed by the whale, and most people recognize that Jonah was an early Christian symbol for Jesus, who was three days dead and returns to life, but after that, details might be a bit sketchy.

Jonah is charged with going to the Ninevites to preach repentance. Now, Jonah doesn't want to do this, not because he fears getting beat up and murdered. Quite the opposite: Jonah hates the Ninevites and he is afraid God will relent and forgive them. So, it's a really bad situation: he'll be helping out his enemies and he will look like a fool since he will have preached fire and brimstone and nothing bad happens. Kind of like those weather people who spend all evening forecasting dire storms only to wake in the morning to a Disney world of bluebirds and sunshine.

Jonah wants to use God as his stick to smash his enemies,

to have God as his personal pit bull to attack those people he does not approve of. He wants God to not like the people Jonah doesn't like. If you're my God, God, don't go around being nice to my enemies. Crush them, like the Psalmist wants. Smash their babies against the rock and all of that, spread salt on their lands, a pox on them and all their generations.

Essentially, Jonah wants to exploit his own relationship with God to his own advantage, and that's the real genius of this story and why it speaks so eloquently to us today. We so want to shape God to our viewpoint and to use him to bring about justice as we understand the term, that is to make us and our opinion prevail. There is a great short story called "The Jilting of Granny Weatherall" by Eudore Welty. (For those younger readers, I always have to explain, as I do to my students, that jilting is leaving someone, dumping them, as for example girls did to me most of my high school dating career.) In that story Granny is dying, but she has no fear because she has this understanding with God. She's already covered. She doesn't even need the consolation of the sacraments at the end, because it has all been paid for in advance. She's got a ticket to heaven. She is, in her mind, the saved. And the story works out that there is no puppet God waiting there at the pearly gates to invite her in. The understanding that she has is not the reality. As in life Granny is jilted here at the end of her life too because she thought to recreate God in her own image and likeness. It's a great story about the tendency we have to make God into the creature we want or need.

Jonah does the same thing. He wants an avenging God, one who will destroy the great city of Ninevah and everyone in it. Teach them a lesson. In this way Jonah resembles so many of us today who are sure we speak for God when we condemn the people we see around us who are clearly sinners. Why God is waiting instead of destroying right now, we're not sure, but we are confident that one day he will pull out his sword of justice and strike down the wicked, leaving a lot more world for us to luxuriate in. All those slackers out there, leading lives of wickedness are one day going to get their comeuppance, just you wait.

And God's answer to Job is so perfect. To me it's one of the finest example of the dangers of our human anthropomorphizing of God, because it gives a great insight into God's point of view. And it happens like this. After the Ninevites repent and are spared, just as Jonah feared would happen, Jonah goes out into the desert to sulk. He finds this great little tree to camp under that it really wonderful. He can sit beneath it in the shade that protects him from the scorching sun. It's been a bad day, but hey, this is a nice consolation prize. But when Jonah goes to sleep that night, God sends a worm to kill the tree, and the next day Jonah becomes even more distraught. One further instance of God disappointing him, not living up to the image Jonah has of what God should be. And as he sits there weeping, God says, "Jonah, you're weeping over a crummy little tree that you liked, and you don't think I should care about a huge city full of my creatures that I love and treasure? Does that make any sense?" Finally the lesson sinks in that God's ways are not Jonah's ways, that the God Jonah created is just that: Jonah's creation and not really God, who is beyond our power to imagine and control.

It is, as I said, a powerful lesson for us during those times when we are tempted (and it is a temptation) to speak for God, to interpret God for the world and manage to project an image of a power that we alone can harness and contain. We alone are able to say who God loves and who God does not. Faith, I have found, is a wonderful thing. It has changed the way I live and the way I view life and other people, but I fear that at times believers get the idea that this faith entitles them to go forth and act as God. This is very different from acting for God, where we are God's hands on earth and do his work in making the Kingdom present in our world. No, acting as God turns us into people who take on the duties of judging others and defining what justice should look like in the world. It makes us into Jonahs and Granny Weatheralls instead of followers of the Way of Jesus.

# 43 WOMAN AT THE WELL

The Gospels present different ways of knowing about Jesus: sayings and reflections and reactions of other people -- but my favorite method is the stories told about him, and no story captures the spirit of Jesus better for me than John's account of him meeting the Samaritan woman at the well. This is one of those long ones that they usually let you sit down for when they read it as the gospel on Sundays, so maybe you remember it but not all of it, so I'll repeat it here for you. If you're like me, you tend to skip poems, songs, and long quotes, but I encourage you to reread this one just because it is so rich in details:

There came a woman of Samaria to draw water. Jesus said to her, "Give me a drink." (For his disciples had gone away intro the city to buy food.) The Samaritan woman said to him, "How is it that you, a Jew, ask for a drink from me, a woman of Samaria" (For Jews have no dealings with Samaritans.) Jesus answered her, "If you knew the gift of God, and who I am that is saying to you, 'Give me a drink,' you would have asked him, and he would have given you living water." The woman said to him, "Sir, you have nothing to draw water with, and the well is deep. Where do you get that living water? Are you greater than our father Jacob? He gave us the well and drank from it himself, as did his sons and livestock." Jesus said to her, "Everyone who drinks of this water will be thirsty again, but whoever drinks of the water I will give him will never be thirsty forever. The water that I will give him will become in him a spring of water welling up to eternal life."

The woman said to him, "Sir, give me this water, so that I will not be thirsty or have to come here to draw water."

Jesus said to her, "Go, call your husband and come here." The woman answered him, "I have no husband." Jesus said to her, "You are right in saying, 'I have no husband', for you have had five husbands, and the one you now have is not your husband.. What you have said is true." The woman said to him, "Sir, I perceive you are a prophet. Our fathers worshiped on this mountain, but you say that in Jerusalem is the place where people ought to worship." Jesus said to her, "Woman, believe me, the hour is coming when neither on the mountain nor in Jerusalem will you worship the Father. You worship what you do not know, we worship what we know, for salvation is from the Jews. But the hour is coming, and is now here, when the true worshipers will worship the Father in spirit and truth." The woman said to him, "I know the Messiah is coming (he who is called Christ). When he comes, he will tell us all things." Jesus said to her, "I who speak to you am he."

I love this story for the many insights into the nature of Jesus and his personality and message.

First of all, he talks to a woman. That in itself doesn't seem like that big a deal, but it was, especially in Jesus' time. Especially alone. Here he is, waiting for his disciples to come back and he strikes up a conversation with someone that he properly should not associate with. She is a woman of unsavory reputation, a fact that he seems to be aware of from the start, and of a different culture altogether. Not the sort of person a great religious figure should be associating with, and yet it doesn't faze Jesus at all. How often in life have we avoided certain people in certain situations just because it might lead to uncomfortable or even embarrassing moments? How often have we been proper over being friendly? And yet, for Jesus, there is none of that. There isn't even a tone of condescension, as if he is looking down on the woman and her situation. When he drops the bomb of knowing that she has been married before, it's more like a statement cutting through any ambiguity rather than a real put down.

Jesus starts out, "Give me a drink." A rather personal request right off. If it were to happen today, Jesus would probably say, "Let me have a drink out of your water bottle." There's an immediate assumption of familiarity with this woman from another background altogether, and the woman responds to that, questioning how Jesus dares to even talk to her.

Besides this forwardness, there's the puzzling dialog on two levels. Jesus starts talking about physical water and then veers off into mystical language about spiritual sustenance through living water, a thread that he continues later with the disciples when he speaks about spiritual food. Whatever our conversation with Jesus over our lifetime is, it is not something we control or totally understand. Jesus always remains for me slightly or a lot enigmatic, always a bit beyond my ken, elusive. He talks to me, but I don't always get it, any more than the woman or the disciples here get it. We understand the words, but they don't make sense, at least they don't make sense in the usual way we have them make sense for us.

There is a dynamic here that is in much of the gospels and in the centuries of dialog of what Jesus is. How did being both God and man play into the everyday Jesus? Here he knows a fact that would seem to correlate with the "super Powered God" nature of Jesus, where he can see and do things no mere mortal can do. And yet, the knowledge he has is not too far beyond what might have been gleaned through listening to various bits of information or observation. It's enough to be interested in the divine and yet not quite in the realm of modern super hero tales. It's not a case of stopping a freight train or seeing through a brick wall, but nevertheless a puzzling piece of information that fits with others, like writing in the sand the sins of those willing to stone the adulterous woman.

It's interesting that in spite of the woman's sinful ways, there is no condemnation aside from an implied one in Jesus' observation, and there is no attempt to convert her explicitly to a "sin no more" way of life. There is however a clear invitation to see Jesus as the fulfillment of the promise for the Messiah, one that she seems to grasp well, returning to the town to spread the message. Jesus meets the woman as she is; there is no attempt to convert her as such. Through it all, the woman remains a fully realized woman, a person with a history and a psychological make-up that comes through the story very well. She changes the topic when Jesus gets too close to the parts of her life that she's not comfortable with and she's curious and bold enough to push Jesus on who he is and why he's acting the way he does. She is no stick figure.

The reaction of the townspeople is unique also. Clearly, many would not be comfortable hearing the words of eternal life uttered by a woman known to be less than salutary in her own life. And so we have those who believe, but also those who go further and believe, not because of second hand knowledge but because of their own first-hand experience of "what we have heard for ourselves." No one else can replace our own experience of Jesus as the Messiah. I'm a lot like some of the townspeople: I can believe if Jesus speaks to me or I personally have experience of his love and life, but if someone I don't care for speaks of Jesus, I'm not very receptive.

But the two great figures in this drama are Jesus and the woman. Jesus just simply approaches this woman as a person. He interacts with her with no preconceptions. She is not a member of a non-believing sect to be converted. She is not an inferior to be talked down to. "Give me a drink of your water bottle." An immediate assumption of kinship. We're here together. You have water; I'm thirsty. Gimme a drink. Away from his disciples, away from any expectations of how a Messiah should act, very straightforward, you and me, just us folks. It's the woman who keeps trying to put everything on a theoretical, theological level: about our fathers, about the Messiah, etc. But these are just dodges, to avoid the uncomfortably personal examination. How have I been living? Who am I living with? Where is my living water? How many times do we escape into the philosophical to avoid the uncomfortable personal truths of our lives? I can do it in a heartbeat.

One final personal note about why I like this passage. I studied Greek for a period in my life. I am embarrassed to tell you this, since I have almost nothing left from those muggy Minnesota summer afternoons spent drooling on a Greek grammar book waiting for recreation time to begin. Being awakened by the kindly Greek teacher checking on my progress politely not remarking on the paper scars on my face from using the textbook as my pillow. Out of that period about the only Greek that has stayed with me is the phrase "*estin bathu*," is deep, as in "the well is deep." Bathos, the word for low comedy, comes from <u>bathu.</u> Not much to claim out of a couple of years of intense Greek study, but it is mine. This has nothing to do with the theological significance of the passage, but I thought I'd pass it along to you anyway as a way of thanking those long gone saints who labored without reward trying to inculcate Latin and Greek into my impermeable mind.

# 44 BIG DEAL

When all is said and done (whatever that means), what sets belief apart from any other way of viewing life? What makes faith different? One concept: Love your enemy. Not love your neighbor, which can be hard enough, depending on where you live and how tightly your block association screens its tenants, but Love your enemy. Love those you already know you can't stand. Love those who seem to go out of their way to annoy, no, to really piss you off. Sorry for the poor language, but you know what I mean, they really get to YOU (and me). Those people, Jesus says, Love them. Not tolerate them, not say they have a right to live, although that is a lot, but to go way beyond that and to say we must love them.

That is a deal breaker.

No wonder so many people walked away from Jesus. Think of the people who are your enemies: on the personal level, on the political level, on the ideological level. In every sense of the term, who are your enemies and why? And how can you possibly love them? It's simply too much to ask, and that's why I think faith, true faith, fuzzy or not, is so hard. Because it's the one injunctive of Jesus that we can't fit into our world view, our way of dealing with everything in our lives. These are bad people. They represent bad things, bad ideas, bad practices. They wish us nothing but harm and how can we defend ourselves against that?

The modern temperament is so far from that concept; it is the polar opposite. Instead of love, the current mindset is to demonize. If someone disagrees with you, it is because he is evil. He is not just someone who has a momentary blind spot, but someone who has a blind spot because he is evil. If we do or think something bad or wrong (a big admission already in our age of certainties) it is because we have had a momentary lapse. We are good people who made a mistake. It's not that we're evil, we just did something wrong.

See the difference? One is just a description of our actions, the other is a definition of our essence. We do things that are wrong although we are basically good; other people do things wrong because they are evil. You can rehabilitate someone who does something wrong, but if they are intrinsically evil, there is no hope except extermination. We see this dynamic at work in our own political system. It is increasingly difficult to galvanize any action toward a bipartisan effort because increasingly each party sees the other, not as a different point of view, but as the evil enemy. How can you make a pact with the devil? And that is what each side sees the other as.

I once taught on the same faculty with a person whom I respected greatly. We were both English teachers with strong personalities and opinions. And we were rarely in agreement. There was almost no topic on which we shared the same per-spective. When it came to an issue at a faculty department meeting I could almost predict what he would think. I just took my own position and then assumed he would have the opposite. And I was usually right.

And yet we got along famously. I genuinely liked him and felt the same in return from him. He was once quoted as say-ing, "Quillin and I agree on almost nothing, a fact that bothers neither of us one bit." I thought that that was the perfect ex-pression of a way to dialog: we could both express our views strongly without fear that it would mean that we had come to a judgment about the other person.

When I moved to a new school, I discovered that almost no one expressed their disagreement directly. Oh, they still har-bored dissenting points of view, but the prevailing atmosphere was that I could not disagree because then people would think I didn't like them. I remember one person saying she liked me because she felt that she didn't have to agree with me, that we could disagree and still be friends. That seems to me to be the bare minimum of civility that holds a society together, and yet Jesus is going way beyond that. He is saying not only do you have to allow the other person her point of view, you have to love her. Even as you abhor and oppose everything about her viewpoint, underneath it you have to love her.

In today's heated context we hate the other political view, we hate ISIS and so on. But in his most radical teaching, Jesus says love your enemy.

And how can we possibly love them?

The answer of faith is that they are also made by God. It is not a Manichean world where some are born evil, but rather a world where all are born into one human family of God, all loved in spite of what we might judge.

Which is all very well to say, but to practice? Oh so difficult. Try it for a minute. Think of the worst person you can imagine. It might be someone you know, but also it could be someone out of the news headlines. It might be a man or woman, but it has to be someone who represents monstrous evil. Picture this person, someone responsible for the deaths of thousands, someone who preyed on the weak and defenseless, someone guilty of the most heinous crimes. There is no redeeming quality in this person. Now, then, say, I love this person. Not just that I can find it in my heart to forgive him or her, but that I love this person. Truly love. Everyday this person makes life unbearable for so many other people, but I love him. Because this person is also a child of God. Pretty hard to say that and really mean it, isn't it? And yet, that is what Jesus is saying when he says love your enemies, do good to those who hate you. You can explain it away how you like, the irreducible bedrock is that Jesus is calling you to something extraordinary.

Who can do that? No wonder Gandhi said Christianity is a nice idea that has never been tried!

Can you accept that challenge Jesus lays before you? Can you love that person? That is the painful question Jesus poses.

And there is nothing fuzzy about the answer we must give to that. Hope is one of the hardest virtues to talk about. It has always been for me, a born and raised skeptic, a difficult topic. It is not easy to define hope without getting into Hallmark cardland. Hope seems to generate reams of sayings and images that tend to make a person ill.

For many years I operated off the assumption that hope was something with feathers until I realized that I hadn't a clue what that meant in spite of loving Emily's poetry. The closest I have come since then to identifying what Christian hope truly is has been through the inchoate meanderings I have done in the theology of Teillard de Chardin. If I understand anything for his writing (and it's quite possible that I don't), it's that all of creation has been altered by Jesus' resurrection. The resurrection gives direction and a goal to all of creation. In spite of how much I loved in my younger years posing as an existentialist who saw only chaos and absurdity in all of the world, I do not believe that now. In spite of the terrible things in politics and in the world among countries and atrocities, I do not believe that the ultimate destiny of the world is destruction.

# 45 FUTURE CATHOLICS

The future of Catholicism? It is fatuous to attempt to predict such a thing, so here goes. I believe that as some of the differences between Catholic and Protestant sects become more and more fuzzy, we will concentrate on the essentials that we understand and hold to be central to our faith. This should lead to more of a realization of what we share instead of what divides us. Some of the old arguments no longer seem as important as the many common elements we hold as Christians. The differences then become matters of individual expressions of our ways of believing instead of identifying points of salvation or perdition.

This is not the same Church I grew up in. Yet, my mother and father would probably have said the same thing. Here is the make or break question: Do I believe the Holy Spirit still guides the Church today? In spite of people I may not have much in common with, do I still believe the Holy Spirit is at work or not? Can I let God lead?

The future of the Catholic Church lies with what Pope Francis, in Gaudete et Exsultate, calls the middle class of holiness, a wonderful phrase that captures the bedrock stratum of faith. These people are and have been always the ones who interpreted and put into practice the various lofty statements emanating from Rome. They are the middle class, not in the sense of mediocrity or faintness of practice, but in the sense of being the moiety of Christians in the world. In their many activities and concerns they demonstrate the principle that Francis calls the "multiplicity of expressions of holiness." The future of Christianity is in the realization and embracing of these various ways of being holy, the letting go of a model that idealizes only the monastic celibate life of the traditional saint and more fully explores the many paths thousands of Christians pursue daily in their journey to be holy.

Along with this changed emphasis is Francis' idea, not new but revolutionary nevertheless, that no one is saved alone. What a wonderful way of looking at things: we are saved as a group. As you influence your family, your friends, your co-workers, your community, so your own salvation will be worked out. As a child of ten, I would have been devastated by the notion that my salvation was dependent on that of my rotten brothers, but now I look at the ramifications of such a theory and am astounded at its brilliance. When we say we are a community of believers, realizing that our salvation is entwined with others gives that idea new importance. We cannot withdraw and work out our salvation in isolation; we are always drawn to be responsible for the welfare of all God's people.

As Pope Francis' vision of Christianity seems to indicate, the future lies not in more laws, but in paring away layers of accretions to the heart of what it means to follow Jesus. All of this sounds to many like -- literally -- heresy, but wasn't part of Jesus' message to cut through some of the needless laws that had come to choke the spirit? Isn't the spirit of following Jesus lost today in some of the codifications casuistries of modern theology? Do we need always to increase our knowledge of Jesus and the meaning of his message? Of course, but at the same time it seems that many of the voluminous rules and laws are drowning the essential meaning of following Jesus in doing the will of his Father. If young and many not so young have lost interest in some of the labyrinthine codices of canon law, perhaps there is something good to come out of this fuzziness. Like an arty portrait that sharpens the image of the person and fuzzes out the background, today's movement of the Spirit may similarly heighten our realization of Jesus and let the remaining detail recede into the faint, fuzzy netherland.

# 46 AMEN

Amen is the easy ending for this book, the clear choice for the last word about faith. Amen always comes at the end of every prayer. At least it did until they started messing with the Our Father. There must have been some kind of compromise at the Vatican where some people wanted to adopt the "Protestant" ending to the prayer and others said ok, but let's put some other prayer in between so it doesn't look like we're caving in completely. So they stuck something between the two parts and made sure no one said Amen after the first part. Which worked ok, I guess, but later when people just said the Our Father by itself sans the new ending, they were no longer trained to say Amen.

But Amen is a great ending for a prayer, a sermon, a book, a life. It says emphatically Yes! It works well as its own prayer. At times I say over and over just the word Amen, Amen, Amen. Yes, Lord, I accept what is here before me. I accept my life. I accept all you have given me.

And so, here, Amen to this book with all its short-comings, may it bring faith and reflection and light to all of you who have persevered to the end. Amen, Amen.

# ABOUT THE AUTHOR

Michael Quillin has taught English and Theology in high schools across the country, from Boston and Jersey City to Milwaukee and Seattle, where he presently resides.

Made in the USA
Coppell, TX
03 December 2019

12331160R00092